THE NEW

Victoria

WALKING GUIDE

THE NEW
Victoria
WALKING GUIDE

Rosemary Neering

Whitecap Books
Vancouver/Toronto/New York

With appreciation to the walkers, Tony and Alma Owen, and especially Bob Harrison and Joe Thompson, who made many good suggestions and wore out their shoes checking the routes in this book. —Rosemary Neering

Whitecap Books
Vancouver/Toronto/New York

Edited by Elaine Jones
Proofread by Elizabeth McLean
Design by Tanya Lloyd/Spotlight Designs
Maps by fennana design
Printed and bound in Canada.

National Library of Canada Cataloguing in Publication Data
Neering, Rosemary, 1945–
    The new Victoria walking guide

    Previous ed. has title: The Victoria walking guide.
    Includes index.
    ISBN 1-55285-184-2

    1. Victoria (B.C.)—Guidebooks.   2. Walking—British Columbia—Victoria—Guidebooks. I. Title. II. Title: Victoria walking guide.
FC3846.I8.N44 2001   917.11'28044   C2001-910531-2
F1089.5.V6N44 2001

The publisher acknowledges the support of the Canada Council and the Cultural Services Branch of the Government of British Columbia in making this publication possible. We acknowledge the financial support of the Government of Canada through the Book Publishing Industry Development Program for our publishing activities.

CONTENTS

Introduction   7

Tour 1:   **Old Town/Chinatown**   9
*Heritage buildings, dim sum and many
a cappuccino.*

Tour 2:   **James Bay**   35
Houseboats, great views and village shops.

Best Places   51
to drink coffee while people-watching

Tour 3:   **Victoria West/Selkirk Water**   53
*Waterfront pubs, harbourfront walkways and
pocket parks.*

Best Places   62
to have a picnic lunch

Tour 4:   **Beacon Hill/Fairfield**   65
*Trees and flowers, pathways and ponds,
waves and graves.*

Best Places   78
*to sit on a bench and contemplate
life (or death)*

Tour 5:   **Rockland**   79
*A crenellated castle, upper-crust houses
and rambling roses.*

Best Places   88
to photograph flowers and trees

Tour 6:   **Oak Bay**   89
            Waterfront walking, eclectic shopping and
            hidden pathways.

            Best Places   102
            with a village atmosphere

Tour 7:   **University of Victoria/Cadboro Bay** 103
            Sprawling rhododendrons, mystical springs
            and a maybe-mythical monster.

            Best Places   112
            to view outdoor art

Tour 8:   **Sidney**   115
            Boats and benches, bronzed statues and books.

            Best Places   123
            to experience lifestyle envy

            Further Information   125

            Index   126

INTRODUCTION

VICTORIA: A CITY FOR WALKERS

It's eight o'clock on a wet and windy Sunday morning, a good time to stay home in the warm and dry. But on Victoria's waterfront, a dozen hardy walkers are striding along the clifftop pathway, and another group is setting out on the breakwater. Across the harbour, parents push a stroller below rain-shiny arbutus trees while two older women finish their morning walk with breakfast at a pathside restaurant.

Victoria is a city meant for walkers. It's blessed with waterfront paths, high on windswept clifftops, along rocky beaches or beside the calmer waters of the harbour. The scale of its downtown is very human: the buildings are low compared to the high-rise jungles of other cities, where soaring towers create wind tunnels and block out the sunshine. In the city's centre, many 19th-century buildings have been preserved, their architecture friendly, filled with stories of the city's past. Here and elsewhere, small shops, coffee houses and pubs invite the passerby to linger.

In the old residential neighbourhoods, many of the heritage houses still stand, restored now to their original colours. These same neighbourhoods cluster around Victoria's villages, the locally owned stores and services that attract the browser, and remind walkers that shopping malls are not the answer to every consumer need.

It's a cliché that Victoria is a city of gardens, but clichés gain currency for a reason. One of the joys of walking urban Victoria is its gardens: English country style with old roses spilling across intentionally untidy flower beds, more formal gardens in the parks and public spaces, beds of lavender and rosemary bordering ocean-side walkways. Here and there are found native plant gardens or the deep blue sweep of flowering camas. Huge trees, native Douglas fir or more exotic imported species, also draw the walker's eye.

Each of the urban walks described in this book has been chosen for the variety it offers. You can rush through each for the exercise — or you can stop for a coffee or a glass of wine, picnic on a bench beside the sea, lunch at a streetside restaurant, browse in village second-hand stores, read stories of a neighbourhood's history in its houses, or succumb to the lifestyle envy brought on by viewing graceful turn-of-the-century mansions or half-million-dollar condominiums with million-dollar views.

At the beginning of each tour description, you'll find the approximate length of time the walk will take, and suggestions for how to reach the start of the tour. Check out, too, the "best of" lists, our picks for some of the most interesting features along the way.

Happy walking.

Walkers on Westsong Way, one of Victoria's many urban walking paths.
(Anton Studios)

OLD TOWN / CHINATOWN

WHAT YOU'LL FIND:
Historic buildings, entertainment, restaurants, coffee houses, souvenir shops, shopping and more shopping, waterfront, people watching.

BACKGROUND:
Downtown Victoria wasn't extraordinarily prosperous in the 1950s and 1960s—and that turned out to be a good thing, because it meant that the area escaped the plague of "tear it down and build a new one" that afflicted many other Canadian cities in those decades. By the time some people were talking about redevelopment, others had awoken to the value of the pleasant heritage streetscape that is the downtown's major attraction.

That streetscape makes the area special for walkers. Unlike in many major cities, buildings are oriented to the sidewalks, and architectural details are very visible. No high-rise wind canyons here: rare is the building that exceeds six storeys.

Which is not to say that Victoria has remained unchanged for half a century. Though some tourist brochures still like to suggest the city is more English than England, you can take that with a mighty grain of salt—or, more likely, with a low-fat latte or barbecued pork bun. Lots of people-watching places here, with outdoor patios for coffee-sipping or lunch-eating; still some eclectic boutiques among the clothing chains that have, inevitably, taken up much of the prime real estate. And there is increasing access to the waterfront.

WATCH FOR:
Street musicians, playing classical music or jazz; more places to drink coffee than you thought possible; interesting architectural

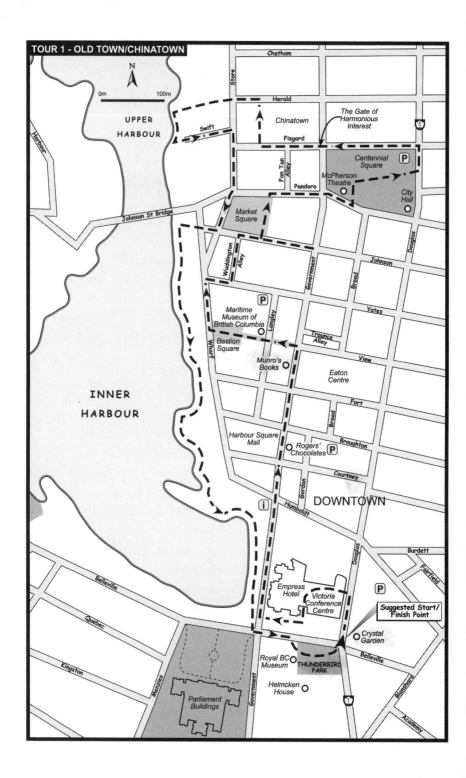

details above street level; passageways (often called alleys) that open off the main street.

TIMING:
If you just walk the route without stopping, it won't take more than an hour. With stops and exploration, it can take most of a day.

TO REACH THE ROUTE:
The tour describes a circle through the downtown-Chinatown area, so can be joined anywhere en route. The city parkade on Yates between Government and Wharf is closest to the tour route. Free, but time-limited (one hour or two) on-street parking is available a few blocks north of Chinatown; three-and-a-half-hour parking is available in Beacon Hill Park, a few blocks south of the tour route. Most buses stop downtown, on Douglas Street or elsewhere nearby.

THE ROUTE:

➤ Begin at the southwest corner (the one with the native longhouse) of Douglas and Belleville streets.

Beside Belleville is Mungo Martin House, named for the Kwakwaka'wakw chief who was the first head carver in the totem restoration program. In the 1940s, northwest coast totems were brought to Victoria for display. As these poles began to deteriorate badly, they were moved to storage. In 1962, native carvers began to create replicas that were raised in Thunderbird Park, behind Mungo Martin House. Among the poles: a Gitxsan memorial pole from the Hazelton area, a Kwakwaka'wakw house post, and a Nuxalk grave figure. In the summer, carvers can often be seen at work here.

➤ Walk north on Douglas across Belleville.

To your right is the Crystal Garden, now a world of tropical monkeys, birds, plants and butterflies, but once the pleasure palace of

Victoria. Built in 1925 on a reinforced concrete raft atop a bog, the garden featured the largest swimming pool in North America. Wrote a commentator then, "under a great canopy of glass... swimmers disport themselves, and on the encircling prom-enade...people chat over tea...while orchestral music floats above the laughter from below." Too expensive to maintain, the pool and dance floor were closed in 1972, and the place was boarded up. But it was rescued and restored in 1980, and lives on today.

➤ About halfway up the block, past the bus station on your left, enter the Victoria Conference Centre through the heavy glass doors at the top of the stairs. Walk through the conference centre hall.

The centre was opened in 1989. Featured inside are paintings and totems; outside, fountains splash in the plaza.

Straight ahead is the Empress Hotel, now titled the Fairmont Empress, long considered the queen of downtown hotels. The Empress is somewhat less receptive to gawkers and walkers than it used to be, possibly because the paying customers resented being on display for passing tourists. The old main front door is now closed off, and it takes the determination of an imperial explorer to get to the main reception lobby from the conference centre. You can

Inside the Victoria Conference Centre.
(Anton Studios)

still, however, stop for a drink or a midday curry in the Bengal Lounge, where an ex-tiger remains pinned to the wall, but the colonial-days-of-Injah service has departed, and the waiters no longer appear to have lived through the days of the Raj.

The lounge began as a reading room for gentlemen residents, then became the first cocktail lounge in Victoria. As the blurb informs us, "whether you are admiring the two extraordinary Punka Fans on the ceiling; observing the rich Mahogany, Teak and Quarter cut oak panelling; gazing at the hand painted silk murals of Utopia India; or relaxing in our comfortable leather sofas enjoying the tastes of the menu, you will be surrounded by the uniqueness of the room." What more can one say?

> Turn left from the convention centre to return outside just before the entrance to the Empress. Continue past the fountain and down the steps or ramp to the driveway. Turn right and walk past the rose gardens on your left to the front of the Empress. Turn right at Government Street and walk along the front of the hotel.

This area was once tidal flats; the causeway that carries Government Street replaced a bridge after the flats were filled. The original part of the hotel was built in 1908 atop pilings driven 38 metres (125 feet) down to bedrock.

Old-timers still remember when the Empress had full-time resident guests during the Depression. Most of them were older people who could barely afford the dollar a night charged for top-floor rooms and who offered bridge and piano lessons to better-off guests. The hotel was refurbished in the 1960s and in 1989, when the new—and to some, very untraditional—lobby was added.

Across Government Street on the causeway sidewalk, Captain James Cook glowers out over the Inner Harbour. Cook sailed into this area in 1778, touching ashore at Nootka on Vancouver Island's west coast, thus becoming the first tourist known to have arrived on

Canada's west coast. Somehow, he failed to stop in at Victoria, probably because no one had yet invented The Butchart Gardens. Behind the statue of Cook are plaques that honour early arrivals in this area and the ships they sailed on. To the north of the statue, at the corner of Government and Wharf across from the Empress, is the Victoria tourist information centre—pop across the street if you want more maps, brochures and information. This building was once a gas station; the lower floors were used for car repair and storage. The 25-metre (82-foot) tower atop the building supports a beacon once visible for a hundred kilometres (60 miles), installed to aid seaplanes arriving after dark—something that didn't happen then and doesn't happen now.

➤ Continue north on Government Street (to your right, away from the Parliament Buildings).

You are now entering the oldest part of Victoria, the streets and buildings that mushroomed out from the fort that was established in 1843. Victoria's metamorphosis began in 1858 when gold panned on the Fraser River arrived in San Francisco. The news spread rapidly and a small army of prospectors and merchants headed north to seek their fortunes. Fort Victoria was an obvious place to make their supply headquarters, and it

Turn-of-the-century architecture along Government Street.

wasn't long before the inevitable tent camp was transformed into a town of brick and stone.

As you cross Humboldt Street, look to your right to see the Union Club building a block away. Like every city with British and Victorian roots, Victoria had its gentlemen's club, this one established in 1879 under the presidency of itinerant judge Matthew Baillie Begbie. "Members have helped to determine the economic and political course of the city, the province and indeed the country," says the club's web site, and the rota of presidents includes senators, members of parliament, doctors, lawyers, military men and sirs. No women, though: the Union Club forbade their membership for more than a century, and gave in only reluctantly when it became clear that no women members meant that fewer men in government and industry would join—a change not universally welcomed among the crusty curmudgeons who frequented the club's dining room and library. In a further bow to economic necessity, the club now advertises its accommodation to all comers, and offers discounts to members of that not so exclusive organization, the American Automobile Association. But if you want to stay, don't forget to pack your tie: some standards must be preserved.

➤ Continue north on Government Street.

The Government Street mall that runs from Humboldt to Yates Street is a compromise. Vehicle traffic is still permitted, but the street is about as vehicle unfriendly as planners can make it, with four-way stops, no on-street parking, and pedestrian crossings that make it difficult for cars to move faster than a crawl (useful in years past when the streetwalkers frequented this area). It is pedestrian friendly, with benches, planters, trees, globe lights, hanging baskets and brick-lined sidewalks.

Though the streetscape of buildings and sidewalks now seems a constant, the occupants of the stores are ever-changing. Back in the 1860s, every brick and stone storefront was occupied by provisioners, saloon keepers and hotel operators. When a recession hit in the 1870s, after the gold rush excitement, bankruptcies and vacancies were the order of the day. The pendulum swing hasn't ceased, though storefronts on the heavily frequented stretch of Government from the Empress to Yates are rarely vacant for long—unless you want to count the ill-advised Harbour Square, an indoor mall that never really caught on in mild-weather Victoria. Now, you'll find coffee emporia, souvenir stores and clothing chains along this strip, together with a few of the old stalwarts that have been here for decades, and, in some cases, for a century or more.

The buildings themselves present a capsule history of the city's economic ups and downs. The Belmont Building, at the corner of Humboldt and Government streets and one of the first in the city of reinforced concrete, is a primary example of what is known as Chicago-style office building. Chicago, notes architectural historian Martin Segger, was the city where modern office buildings were invented. Construction of the Belmont started in 1912, when it seemed that prosperity would go on forever. Intended as a hotel, it was delayed by the recession of 1912–13 and the First World War, and completed as an office building after the war.

At the northeast corner of Government and Courtney, 901 Government may be the oldest remaining brick building in town—though the bricks don't show through the mock-Tudor front. Built in 1858 as the Victoria Hotel, surviving through the 1890s as the Windsor Hotel, it was gussied up in the 1930s with the first tourist campaign to promote Victoria as a little bit of olde Englande—a decision that the city just can't get rid of. That it exists at all is probably at least partly due to the fact that it was built of brick not wood, unusual in those early days of "throw it up and start counting the money." When gas mains were installed on the street, the hotel owner went looking for a gas leak, lighting his way with a candle. Not a good idea: the gas exploded, the interior was wrecked and the owner was badly singed.

The odd-numbered side of the 900-block Government, between Courtney and Broughton streets, presents a pleasant 1890s streetscape, with a variety of architectural influences. At 913 Government is a Victoria institution, Rogers' Chocolates. Now that these rich chocolates are sold from Newfoundland to New York, you can no longer identify a real Victorian by his or her knowledge of Rogers Creams. But that's okay: we can share—though some of us get a little impatient when we drop by to buy one of the big cream chocolates and have to wait in line behind a variety of tourists dithering over whether to get Aunt Maude the dark chocolate creams or the mixture of caramels and nuts. The inside of the store is worth a look, even if chocolates are off your list of temptations; check out the leaded glass, mosaic-tile floor and oak panelling.

Charles Rogers and his wife Leah opened this shop in 1916. After the couple's only son shot himself, the Rogers grew increasingly eccentric. They lived behind the shop, starting each chocolate-making day well before dawn, choosing who they would sell to and how many chocolates each could have. After Charles died, Leah gave away most of the Rogers' money, and lived on a small pension until she died 25 years later.

The retail store that occupies the lower floor of the Weiler Building, at 921 Government, carries on a merchandising tradition that began in the 1890s with Otto Weiler, who set himself up as the purveyor of the exotic, the fashionable and the expensive. Victoria's first department store offered art glass, silverware, textiles, Turkish carpets and every variety of dry goods. Featured was furniture from the Weiler factory around the corner. Huge timbers support the five-storey building, and the high arched windows are still visible. Take a look inside to see some of the original woodwork.

Look down at the sidewalk between Broughton and Fort Street to see bricks inlaid to show the original outline of Fort Victoria; they bear the names of Victoria pioneers. Before the often rude and crude gold-rushers appeared upon the scene, Victoria was a genteel outpost of empire despite its association with the rough-and-ready fur trade. The fur-trading fort was established in 1843 when it looked likely that the Americans would take over the Hudson's Bay Company headquarters on the Columbia River. It was far enough removed from the regions where furs were actually acquired, and in a serene enough climate, that it attracted gentlemen and ladies who enjoyed a relaxed and thoroughly English style of life that the gold rush completely disrupted.

From Broughton to Fort, and continuing along the west side of Government to View, you'll find a number of heritage buildings, including the following.

- 1001 Government, the Hamley Building, 1870 (third and fourth floors added in 1887)
- 1007 Government, 1009-1013 Government, built about 1870
- 1017 Government, ca. 1880, once the Albion Hotel
- 1002 Government, Pemberton Holmes Building, 1899
- 1006 Government, Warner Building, 1905
- 1012 Government, Buccaneer Building, date unknown
- 1022 Government, Bank of British Columbia, 1883

Along this row, look for Italianate features, such as round-headed windows and decorative rooflines adapted from styles popular in San Francisco, whence came many of Victoria's prosperous 1890s merchants.

Early Victoria's banks were all in a row on Government Street, and all now serve other purposes: a Christmas store, a bookstore, several clothing stores. The Bank of British Columbia building at the southwest corner of Government and Fort streets was the first on the scene, in 1886. This Renaissance Italian building features a splayed-corner entrance and other design features whose origins architectural historians trace back to the great banking city of Florence in early Renaissance times. Robert Service, the bard of the Yukon gold rush, worked here for $50 a month before he fled north, sleeping in an apartment above a trapdoor to the vault, with a loaded revolver on the bedside table. He was, he wrote, to "wake up at the smallest noise, to pop off possible burglars.... after the first week, it would have taken a charge of nitroglycerine to arouse me." Service brought in a piano, bought a dinner jacket and made the round of parties, dances, theatre and golf, resolving to abandon his dreams of adventure for life as a "nice fat little banker." Fortunately for us, and for Dangerous Dan McGrew and his ilk, he changed his mind.

The 1909 Royal Bank building now houses Munro's Books, surely one of the most elegant bookstores anywhere. Pop inside to peruse the shelves, and take a look upwards at Carol Sabiston's fabric banners. The stone Bank of Montreal building (1896) at the corner of Government and Bastion Square hearkens back to the château style of Canadian Pacific Railway hotels—and so it should, for the Bank of Montreal backed the railway and came west with it. Across from the old Bank of Montreal building is the 1912 Union Bank building at 1205 Government. All these banks closed their Government Street branches in the 1980s.

Murchie's Tea and Coffee is a Vancouver institution (founded in 1894) that moved to Victoria in the 1960s, and switched sides of the street when the Eaton Centre was built. You could have a double decaf lo-fat latte here—but why would you, when you could sample Imperial White Silver Needles or Green Snail Spring Pido Chun tea from China? If your taste is more conventional, try one of the blends Murchie's makes for the Empress Hotel or Craigdarroch Castle. If you need your coffee-fix, you can always munch on some chocolate-covered coffee beans from the retail store beside the tea and coffee bar.

Just past Murchie's at 1116 Government Street is Morris Tobacconists, a hold-over from a much less tobacco-hostile Victoria. You can go in to see the eternal flame on the gas jet of the Mexican onyx electrolier, for the convenience of cigar smokers—but you can't light your cigar, since smoking in public buildings is forbidden in Victoria. Have a look too at the walk-in cabinet for cigar storage, the mahogany panelling and the mirrors on ceiling and walls.

An employee demonstrates the cigar lighter at Morris Tobacconists. If he actually lights his cigar, he'll be in violation of Victoria's strict anti-smoking law. (Anton Studios)

Across the street is the newly revitalized Eaton Centre—or should that be *eaton centre*, given the typography of the reborn department store? There was a good deal of controversy when the Eaton Centre was being planned in the late 1980s, as heritage purists protested the destruction of a number of old-town buildings. The new structure eventually combined heritage facades with new buildings in the four-level mall and six-storey building. What neither side could have predicted was the collapse of one of Canada's mainstays, the chain of Eatons department stores that had served the nation for decades. Merchants north of the new centre complained that their territory became a black hole with the building of the mall; now the centre itself seemed ready to become part of that hole. Fortunately, the Victoria store was one of just a handful across the country chosen by new owner Sears to carry a new eatons banner, reopening late in 2000.

➤ At the corner of Government and View, turn left towards Bastion Square. (Look for the plaque on the front of 69 Bastion Square, corner of Government and Bastion.) Walk through to Langley Street. Cross the street and continue into the main part of Bastion Square.

Originally a street, then a parking lot, the wide walkway to Wharf Street was converted to a square featuring retail outlets in the late 1960s, with refurbishment of its heritage buildings continuing on through the 1990s. Entrepreneur, MLA and historian/author Sam Bawlf—who has recently startled northwest coast historians with well-supported claims about an early visit by Sir Francis Drake to the coast—was largely responsible for this, the first of the old town restorations.

If Germany comes to mind when you view the turreted cream-and-blue-trimmed building that houses the Maritime Museum of British Columbia, on your right as you enter the square, your instincts are on target. The design for what was the provincial courthouse from 1899 to 1962 is probably based on a courthouse in the architect's native Munich. An ornate open-cage elevator, said to be the oldest operational elevator in British Columbia, was installed because a chief justice had been warned by his doctor not to climb stairs.

Building of this courthouse postdates the last public hanging in Victoria, which took place in Bastion Square in the 1880s, when Charlie Rogers was hanged for killing a fellow prison guard in New Westminster.

The Maritime Museum, open every day except Christmas, houses a multitude of maritime-related exhibits, including the *Tilikum*, mariner John Voss's modified cedar dugout

Autumn in Bastion Square.

canoe, in which he planned to circumnavigate the world. He didn't quite make it: three years and three months after he left Victoria in 1901, he arrived in Margate, England, to end his voyage. Exhibited at Earls Court in 1905, the canoe was later sold, then discovered lying derelict in 1929. It was crated and returned to Victoria, where it was restored.

Picture Thomas John Burnes, striding through the square in his trademark black cape, top hat and gold-knobbed cane, greeting friends and acquaintances on all sides. Burnes was a saloon keeper in pioneer Victoria, foreman of the volunteer firefighting Tiger Company. On the north side of the square past the museum, the red brick Burnes House, built in 1887, was Burnes's pride and joy. The hotel thrived for a few years, but the smallpox epidemic of 1892 scared away many a mariner, and the hotel was converted into offices. In 1930, it became a warehouse—though it possibly also housed a brothel. The building was restored in 1967.

Across the square is the former Law Chambers building, built in 1899 and convenient to the courthouse; the 1892 stone and brick Board of Trade Building is at 31 Bastion Square.

A redesign intended to rid the square of the homeless has not been entirely successful, but has opened up the view out over the harbour. Check the lower floors of the buildings for antiques, high-end garden supplies and restaurants.

> Continue through Bastion Square down to Wharf Street, facing the harbour, and turn left (south).

From the earliest days of commercial Victoria, Wharf was the warehouse district and home to saloons and hotels that were the sailors' first place of call on arrival in town. At the corner of Bastion Square, 1129 Wharf, is one of the earliest, built in 1861. At the entrance, look for a caduceus, the herald's wand carried by Hermes (Mercury), the messenger of the gods who also served as the Greek god of commerce.

This warehouse and the ones next door at 1107–1121 Wharf housed the wholesale operations of pioneer merchant R.P. Rithet and were also built in 1861. The Rithet Building, 1117 Wharf, was beautifully restored in 1977 to house the provincial tourism department. Workmen discovered and restored an old well at the back of the main lobby.

➤ Retrace your steps towards Bastion Square, and continue north on Wharf Street.

On both sides of Wharf north of Bastion Square are more warehouses and commercial buildings that date to the period from 1860 to 1900. The buildings at 1205–1213 Wharf have for many decades been merchants' spaces: in the nineteenth century, they housed such business as a smithy, a dry-goods merchant and a wheelwright. Now they are home to restaurants, art galleries and a changing group of other merchants who cater mostly to the tourist trade.

Across the street at 1218 Wharf is the earliest surviving building on Wharf Street. This stone structure, which can be seen best from the water side, began as a saloon and liquor warehouse. It's had its ups and downs: various restaurants have tried to make a success of upstairs and downstairs, but the huge airy space is difficult to manage.

➤ Continue north on Wharf Street, cross Yates, and turn right on Yates.

The 500-block of Yates contains a fine selection of brick and stone buildings, with iron pillars and decorative details that date from the 1880s and the 1890s. The 1895 building at 570 Yates is still a hotel, maintaining its use through many an incarnation. Look for the stylized lions that stare out from the foliage carved on the pillars of one of these buildings. The 1887 Boucherat Building at 533 Yates was built for liquor merchants, and later housed Turkish sulphur baths.

➤ Turn into Waddington Alley, between 518 and 524 Yates.

Spare a glance for the International Hostel Building at 516–518 Yates, in what must be one of the best locations in the world for low-rent tourist accommodation. On your right is the 1896 Leiser Building, built by wholesale grocer Simon Leiser. Leiser installed two lines of track on each floor, leading to an elevator that contained a turntable, so that freight could be loaded or unloaded in either direction.

Waddington Alley is the last place in the city where you will see wooden paving blocks. Not the originals, though—the city has repaved the alley with facsimiles of the creosote-impregnated blocks that decades ago muffled the sound of horses' hooves as they drew carriages through the city streets. On your right is the original premises of Morley's Soda Water Factory. A nineteenth-century Victoria entrepreneur, Christopher Morley (no, not that Chris-

Building details along Waddington Alley.

topher Morley!), produced soda water, lemonade, essences of peppermint and ginger and many other concoctions blended to soothe the city's non-alcoholic thirst.

➤ Continue through Waddington Alley to Johnson Street.

It was Wille's Bakery, not Willie's Bakery as the sign suggests, named for pioneer miller and baker extraordinaire Louis Wille, who fed Victoria's need for bread and pastries from 1887 on. The restoration of historic buildings on Johnson Street has reclaimed one of Victoria's more charming streetscapes—even if charming was not the word one might use to describe the original line of hotels, brothels and saloons that attracted male visitors and, one must suppose, even supposedly staid residents of the city.

➤ Turn right on Johnson Street, and walk up the south side of the street.

The buildings in the first half of the block were run-down until restoration by old-town hero Michael Williams, who died in 2000. Before restoration, lower Johnson contained a hodgepodge of second-hand stores where treasures often lurked amid dross; now the stores are trendier, though some still sell second-hand goods. The building at 541–545 Johnson began life in 1892 as the Colonial Metropole Hotel (owner Thomas Tugwell added the "Metropole" to his hotel's name, presumably to convey Victoria's status as a metropolis, as well as her links with the Olde Countrye). Other buildings in this strip went up between 1880 and 1892. The Paperbox Arcade leads to a restaurant with a brick-walled patio.

➤ Continue up Johnson to Government, past a series of turn-of-the century buildings, cross Johnson, and turn back down the north side of Johnson towards the water.

Ahead and to your right is Market Square. The restoration of the buildings on Johnson Street and the development of Market Square enlivened this area of the old town. Though the stores of Market Square have perhaps not been as successful as their owners might have liked, it's a space unlike any other in Victoria: three storeys of arcades and heritage storefronts that deserve to be far better known than they are. You can buy a slab of fudge here, a quilting square, a book on art, a record, vegetarian or Mexican nosh, clothing from around the world. In summer, you can sit on the benches in the quadrangle and listen to jazz or folk performers at festival time, or hear the buskers who find this a good acoustical space—though probably not a profitable one—or sign up for kayaking lessons.

The Johnson Street side of Market Square presents one of the most attractive heritage lineups of the town. The brightly painted Strand Hotel building (562–564) replaced the Strand Café and a brothel in 1892. The Milne Block (560) opened as a hotel in 1891. Owner A.R. Milne was the controller of Chinese entry for the port of Victoria. Next door is the former Drake Hotel, built in 1894.

➤ Turn from Johnson Street into Market Square.

The fountain at the square entrance had its origins as a horse and dog watering trough—something dogs still seem to sense on a hot summer's day.

➤ Descend to the lower level of the square.

A ravine and creek once ran between Johnson and Pandora streets, dividing white Victoria from Chinatown. From the lower level, look east, towards a parking lot, where you will see what remains of the ravine.

➤ Wander around the square, emerging eventually on the north side, onto Pandora Street.

The restored buildings facing Pandora Street replaced wooden huts that housed Chinese immigrants until the late 1880s and shops, such as one occupied by an opium merchant.

➤ Turn right, away from the water, and head up Pandora Street. Cross Government, cross Pandora, and enter Centennial Square.

Probably the least successful of Victoria's public spaces, Centennial Square may once have been the most crowded: it was the city's marketplace. The history of theatre on this corner dates back to 1914. In 1917, Alexander Pantages opened the Orpheum Theatre with Miss Ethel Armstrong and her fourteen Armstrong baby dolls, two comedy teams (one in blackface), a juggler and a stage and silent-screen star.

Legends swirl around Pantages: perhaps his fortune grew from his early days in the Yukon, where he is said to have separated gold dust from the sawdust he swept from a saloon floor. In Victoria he worked as a café cook, then somehow managed to open, one by one, the largest chain of vaudeville theatres in North America. But the new movies that were soon appearing on theatre screens doomed his live performances. Depressed and ill, he is said to have taken to a semi-dark room in Victoria, where he summoned violinists to play mournful tunes.

Owner Thomas Shanks McPherson willed the building to the city in the 1960s. It was added to and substantially remodelled, with a baroque revival interior that features plaster cherubim—something that undoubtedly pleases the ghost of Alexander Pantages. It is now the McPherson Theatre, one of the city's main performance spaces.

Have a look in Centennial Square at the fountain, its surrounds bearing a striking resemblance to egg cartons, and at the Elizabethan Revival Knot Garden. Angry citizens annoyed at their high tax levels—does anything ever change?—halted construction on the first wing of City Hall in 1878, but this was completed, as were subsequent wings in 1881 and 1891. The clock, with four 225-kilogram (496-pound) dials and a 984-kilogram (2,170-pound) bell, was installed in 1891, after circumnavigating the globe: it was sent first from England to the state of Victoria in Australia.

➤ Leave Centennial Square on the east side, exiting onto Douglas Street. Turn left (north). Proceed to Douglas and Fisgard; cross Fisgard and turn left (west.)

The Hudson's Bay Company that founded Victoria is long gone from this town; all that remains is The Bay, a store that came up with the advertising slogan "Shopping is good." The Bay building on the northeast corner of Douglas and Fisgard was under construction in 1914, put on hold for the years of World War I and completed in 1921. Legions of shoppers have, presumably, been Doing Good there ever since.

Practise up on your secret handshake: at the northwest corner of Fisgard and Government is a Masonic Temple, built in 1878. Architect John Teague, who forswore prospecting in the Cariboo for the city life of architecture, was one of two Masons who bid to design the temple. Good career move: he won the bid, took over from his rival as grand superintendent of works, became grand master of Victoria's Masonic lodge, then mayor of Victoria. He also designed the first wing of City Hall, among a number of other public buildings.

➤ Continue west on Fisgard Street.

Across the street is the old police station, dating from 1920 and replaced by a larger, much more modern station on Caledonia Street in the 1990s. It's said that the cells here were made by the same people who built the cells at Alcatraz.

Set back from the right-hand side of the street is the Chinese School, a direct result of anti-Oriental prejudice against the city's Chinese-Canadian community around the turn of the century. In 1907, a city ordinance commanded that only Canadian-born Chinese children could attend public school. The Chinese Consolidated Benevolent Association, who had already lost a court suit challenging a previous exclusionary ruling, determined to build their own school. The Zhinghua Xuetang (Chinese Imperial School) opened in 1909 with classes in English and Chinese. Now that Canadians of Chinese heritage are thoroughly integrated into public schools, the Chinese School offers after-school classes, to anyone of any age or origin, in Chinese language and arts. The building itself is an interesting combination of western and Oriental forms.

Although the gate demarcating Chinatown is half a block away, Chinatown begins here, stretching west to Store Street and a block north and south. This area was the heart of the Forbidden City, where Chinese felt at home and whites rarely entered. Nineteenth- and early twentieth-century Chinatown was a maze, mysterious to the white man, of opium dens, tenements and gambling houses that catered to the largely male population of the area. Many Chinatown buildings were erected by tongs, groups of people with the same last name, from the same region of China, or speaking the same dialect. The tongs provided a sense of family for the men who emigrated to Canada.

The beautifully restored building at 622–626 Fisgard was erected by the Gee Tuck Tong in 1903. Next door is the Lee Ben Association Building, dating from 1911. These buildings and others nearby display some of the characteristic architecture that joins Chinese and western outlooks: cheater storeys—mezzanines installed between the first and second floors, to cheat the tax collector who based assessments on floor space; recessed balconies that offered a vantage point for street-watching and protected residents from sun and heat in summer, cold in winter; traditional colours of red for happiness, gold for wealth, yellow for the imperial power of China, and green for peace, growth and harmony.

➤   Continue west on Fisgard Street, across Government.

The Gate of Harmonious Interest, *Tong Ji Men*, was erected in 1981 to mark co-operation between Chinese Canadians and the rest of the community, and Chinese participation in the community. The supernatural creatures on the gate symbolize the quadrants of the heavenly vault in Chinese mythology: the azure dragon, the representative of the great celestial power and of the yang, or male, element of the universe; the vermilion phoenix, representing the yin, or female, element; the white tiger; and the black tortoise. The stone lions at the base of the gate were donated by Victoria's sister city, Suzhou, in Jiangsu Province, China.

You probably won't hear the clacking of mah-jong tiles or the hubbub of male voices exhorting the gods for luck, but the ghosts are there: the playing of fan tan—a game where the player guesses how many will be left over when a pile of sticks is divided into four—pai gow and thirteen cards long outlived Chinatown's existence as a purely Chinese enclave. Gambling clubs continued to operate into the 1990s. Interestingly, when a casino was proposed for Chinatown in the late 1990s, a number of Chinese Canadians were strongly opposed, citing both the damage that gambling can do to individuals and families, and the stereotype of Chinese as gamblers. Fan Tan Alley, on the left halfway down the block, was one of the narrow passageways to the Forbidden City; it and others

Street scene in Chinatown.

allowed the residents to control entrance to the area and to escape if the police came to raid the opium dens and gambling clubs.

Few Chinese Canadians live in Chinatown today. The old men who were its primary residents have died or moved to care homes. The main residents now are artists living, not always legally, in small upstairs studios.

Take a look as you walk through Chinatown at the exotic fruits and vegetables available, and stop in for some barbecued pork, noodles or ginger crab.

➤ Halfway down the north side of the block, check to see whether Dragon Alley at 532½ Fisgard is open. If it is, enter the passageway and proceed through it to Herald Street.

If Dragon Alley is closed, continue to Store Street, at the end of the block, and turn right. Continue to Herald Street.

Dragon Alley and the buildings that line it are part of the labyrinth behind the main streets of Chinatown, a labyrinth where hundreds of Chinese men lived. Recently opened, this passageway contains apartments and offices that house alternative health practitioners, artists and others who are attracted by the ambience. The second floor of the building at the end of the passageway, 539 Herald Street, was—what else?—a bordello. The arched doorways in the building suggest its early use as livery stables and carriage repair shop, a use echoed in the 1990s when it was a storage area for Tally-Ho tourist-tour carriages.

➤ Turn left on Herald, and continue to Store Street at the end of the block.

To your right across Store Street are the buildings housing Capital Iron, where decades of Victorians have gone to find hardware gizmos and marine equipment available nowhere else in town. The main floor and basement of 1900 Store Street date back to 1867;

extra storeys were added later and a flour and rice mill operated in the building until 1923. Vacant for a time, it then housed the scrap metal operation that evolved into Capital Iron. Former newspaper boy and ships' dishwasher Morriss Greene ran the business here for almost 40 years, dismantling some 100 ships and thus acquiring a vast stock of ships' chandlery. A travelling steam crane was in use until 1972, the year Greene died.

> ➤ Cross Store Street, and continue along Herald Street
> towards the water. Walk down the steps to your left at the
> end of the street (follow sign for the Canoe Club), and
> turn left in front of the Canoe Club.

The Canoe Club is a brew pub; sample some of its ales and lagers as you sit outside overlooking the Upper Harbour or inside contemplating the huge timbers that support this former warehouse. In season, you can also catch one of the bustling little harbour ferries here, to travel back to the Inner Harbour or up the Gorge waterway.

> ➤ Past the pub, turn left up Swift Street. Cross Store Street.
> Turn right, and continue along Store.

Swan's Hotel, on your left, is a beautifully restored building—also by Michael Williams—that houses a brew pub and restaurant; you can compare its brews with those at the Canoe Club, then stagger back to the tour starting point. On your right is the nearly derelict Janion Hotel; stories swirl about the elderly owner who doesn't want to sell the building, and about the amount of money it would take to restore this heritage-registered building.

> ➤ Cross Pandora. The waterfront street jogs past Market
> Square, and becomes Wharf Street. Cross Johnson Street,
> then cross Wharf, towards the water, at the crosswalk.
> Follow the pathway ahead down to the water, then veer
> to the left to follow the walkway along the water.

The Johnson Street Bridge lifts to allow passage to a tug and barge.

Past the modern hotel on your left are the random-rubble foundations of the buildings that front on Wharf Street. When you reach the parking lot, you'll see at the steep rise to Wharf Street the outlines of old bricked-up arches in the former Hudson's Bay warehouses; the arches allowed entry to below-street storage.

➤ Continue along the waterfront walkway, past some of the most expensive boats to visit Victoria.

Look for these luxury yachts, which sometimes carry helicopters on their decks and movie stars in their elegant staterooms. The bright pink building on your left past the end of the parking lot is the 1874 Customs Building.

➤ Follow the walkway up and down stairs and into the next parking lot.

Continue along the water's edge, and continue south along the walkway, where you'll often find mimes, musicians and artists.

➤ Climb the stairs at the south end of the harbour, to reach the corner of Government and Belleville streets. Cross Government, cross Belleville. Turn left on Belleville.

On your right is the carillon tower, built in 1967 as a gift to British Columbia by people of Dutch origin who live in the province. The belfry contains 49 bronze bells cast in Holland; 75 stairs wind through six complete circles to the carillonneur's position. The bells sound the quarter hours and bell music is played at noon. Behind and below the tower is the Provincial Archives of B.C. Take a look in the lobby to see whether there are any old photographs displayed. Native plant gardens border the pond at the entrance.

➤ Continue east past the main museum building.

The Royal British Columbia Museum is known worldwide for its innovative displays. The First People's Gallery, the modern history gallery and the natural history gallery, as well as an IMAX theatre, are features of the museum.

➤ Continue past the outdoor display cases that house totems and house fronts from coastal villages, and turn right to go up the paved incline beside the museum.

This path leads to Helmcken House and St. Ann's Schoolhouse, both historic buildings. Helmcken House is probably the oldest house on its original site in Victoria; it was built in 1852 for John Sebastien Helmcken, pioneer doctor and politician. The school-house is thought to have been built about 1845 by Hudson's Bay Company employees as a cabin. It then served as the school for the Sisters of St. Ann, some of whose members came to Victoria in 1858.

➤ Return through the totem park behind these historic build-ings to the corner of Douglas and Belleville, the starting point of this tour.

JAMES BAY

WHAT YOU'LL FIND:
Waterfront, heritage houses, fish and chips, houseboats, fishing boats, great views.

BACKGROUND:
James Bay, bordered by the water on three sides, Beacon Hill Park on the fourth, is one of Victoria's most popular and most varied residential areas. Here you'll find old houses divided into single-room rentals not far from some of the city's most expensive water-front condos. Stop by the village shopping area, and you'll notice green-haired, body-pierced young people jumping aside for high-speed seniors on motorized scooters. Though it has a reputation for a fairly high property crime rate, it's also friendly and garden-filled.

This was the second area of the city to be developed. The site of the Hudson's Bay Company farm from 1843 to about 1853, James Bay was divided into four-hectare holdings. Prominent people, including James Douglas, the governor of Vancouver Island, built their homes here, across the Inner Harbour from Fort Victoria. It was originally separated from the downtown area by a somewhat rank mudflat that was filled in around the turn of the century; the causeway in front of the Empress Hotel then replaced the bridge that linked the two parts of the town.

Over time, James Bay acquired two other roles: the Parliament Buildings and subsequently many of the functions of the colonial, then the provincial, government were based here; and the wharves along the Inner and Outer Harbour attracted industrial development.

Some of the stately houses remain, along with many smaller cottages erected when James Bay became a working-class neighbourhood

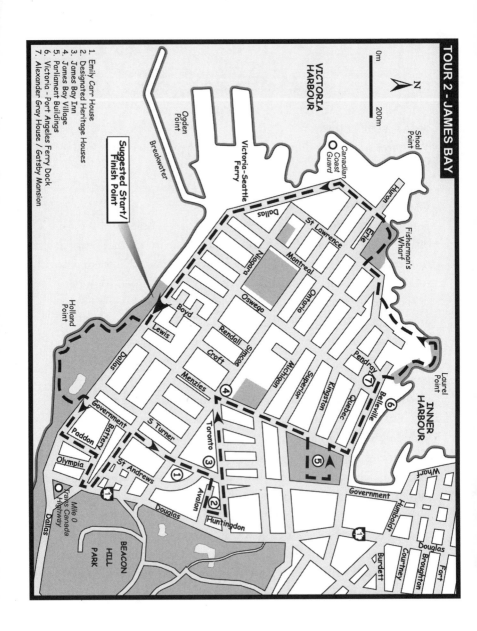

TOUR 2 - JAMES BAY

VICTORIA HARBOUR

Shoal Point

Canadian Coast Guard

Ogden Point

Breakwater

Victoria-Seattle Ferry

Fisherman's Wharf

Dallas
St Lawrence
Niagara
Montreal
Ontario
Oswego
Superior
Michigan
Kingston
Quebec
Erie
Turner
Pendray
Belleville
Laurel Point

Holland Point

Boyd
Lewis
Rendall
Simcoe
Croft
Menzies

INNER HARBOUR

Dallas

Government
Battery
S Turner
Paddon
Toronto
Avalon
Huntingdon

Olympia

St Andrews
Douglas

Mile 0
Trans Canada Highway

Dallas

BEACON HILL PARK

Wharf

Government

Humboldt
Douglas
Burdett
Courtney
Broughton
Fort
Burdett

Suggested Start/ Finish Point

1. Emily Carr House
2. Designated Heritage Houses
3. James Bay Inn
4. James Bay Village
5. Parliament Buildings
6. Victoria - Port Angeles Ferry Dock
7. Alexander Gray House / Gatsby Mansion

N

0m   200m

as wealthier residents moved to areas such as Rockland and Oak Bay. The Parliament Buildings are still a major attraction, but most of the industrial and wharf activities have been replaced, especially along the Inner Harbour, by tourist attractions and accommodations, as well as by waterfront condominium developments.

WATCH FOR:

Intentionally unkempt English cottage gardens, scuba divers, politicians and tourists, wedding parties at the fancy hotels.

TIMING:

The route covers about eight kilometres (five miles) with nary a hill in sight. A 90-minute walk; a half-day adventure, with time for looking at heritage, enjoying the view, eating, drinking and watching the passing parade. Mostly flat; steps up and down to the beach, which can be avoided if you stay on the top of the cliffs.

TO REACH THE ROUTE:

This tour follows a circle route, so walkers can join it anywhere en route. The tour description begins on Dallas Road. The best parking is along Dallas Road, between the breakwater and Government Street, where there are no time limits. Most other streets en route have time-limited parking (usually one or two hours) or are restricted to resident parking. By bus: take the #5 Beacon Hill bus to James Bay, or walk the few blocks from downtown (served by many bus routes) to Belleville Street, and pick up the tour route there.

THE ROUTE:

> ➤ Begin your walk on the south (ocean) side of Dallas Road, between Boyd and Lewis streets. Opposite Lewis Street, bear right from the sidewalk onto the path that leads along the cliffs above the water.

Along the seawall on Dallas Road. (Anton Studios)

Once a major hazard to ships entering the harbour, Brotchie Ledge, identified by a white and green marker offshore, hasn't claimed any victims recently. It serves as a landmark for sports fishers who prowl for salmon in season.

This area was for many centuries home to the Lekwammen people, who lived in a fortified village atop the cliffs, with semi-circular earthworks and a wooden stockade strategically placed so watchers could see any enemy—or friend—approaching across the Strait of Juan de Fuca.

Then as now, the cliff along which you walk is subject to erosion; the Lekwammen name for the area translates as "falling away cliffs." That erosion gave rise to much controversy in the 1990s, as those who wanted to keep the cliffs from disappearing millimetre by millimetre argued with those who wanted no human interference with nature's processes. The interventionists won. By terracing, planting and placing special netting that would disintegrate once the plants took hold, they instituted a non-intrusive solution.

➤ Follow the path to the marker for Holland Point, and go down the steps to the beach. Continue along the beach past the marker for Fonyo Beach.

Steve Fonyo tried to follow the much-praised run of his hero Terry Fox. Fonyo did make it across Canada, but his problems with life afterwards have tended to overshadow his remarkable achievement.

➤ Return up a second set of steps to the clifftop, and turn left on the path.

The thickets of trees and bushes along the waterfront have been swept into a sideways quiff by the strong winds that blow off the strait.

➤ Just after the two-kilometre marker, turn right between two thickets, to reach Harrison Yacht Pond.

The pond was built in the 1950s. Though for many years it was home to more birds than boats, the Victoria model boat society has become more active over the last few years, and a visit to the pond on a Sunday morning will reveal all manner of craft, from sardine-can sailboats, to meticulously crafted sailing ships, motorized yachts and whole miniature flotillas.

A model boat enthusiast takes his boat for a walk at Harrison Yacht Pond.

➤ Bear left around the yacht pond to Dallas Road. Cross
Dallas Road, and turn right. Turn left on Paddon Street.

Many a cottage was built around the turn of the century in James
Bay, and many a workman and his family came to live in them. Some
of these small houses were built as rental property, an investment
for widows that provided an annuity for them. The houses at 23, 26
and 32 Paddon were built in 1903.

High above these cottages, you'll see the turret of a house of an
entirely different type. Pinehurst, built in 1890, commanded much
of the surrounding land running down to the waterfront from here.
American lumber baron William Macauley and his brother
Alexander, and their wives, who were sisters, occupied this 18-room,
18-fireplace (and undoubtedly less than 18-bathroom) mansion after
Macauley retired here. The Macauleys moved out to Rockland, and
a prominent doctor moved in. In time, and like many of the older
mansions in James Bay, Pinehurst fell into disrepair and was threatened with demolition. Fortunately, it became the centrepiece for a
Capital Regional District housing development.

➤ Turn right on Battery Street.

Though no other dwelling near here approaches the splendour of
Pinehurst, a cluster of houses on Battery Street is worth a look. The
house at 638 Battery (ca. 1910) was first occupied by a railway con-
ductor; 642 (ca. 1893) by a civil servant (take a look at the "breakfast balcony"); 648 also by a civil servant, a compositor with the
provincial printing department; 651 (ca. 1913) by a realtor; 670 by an
organist/choirmaster; and 674–676 by a railway agent.

➤ Turn left on Douglas Street.

To your right is Mile Zero of the Trans-Canada Highway, the cairn
often surrounded by gaggles of picture-taking tourists who rush off
and on tour buses.

> Turn left on Niagara Street and follow it back to Government, past more turn-of-the-century houses and much more recent apartment and condominium blocks. Turn right (north) on Government Street.

Signs that advertise rooms or apartments for rent or bed-and-breakfast establishments along Government Street suggest that few of the stately older houses remain single-family dwellings. Many were converted to boarding houses or apartment buildings decades ago, some more recently into condominiums. Though many of these larger houses were once run-down, you'll notice as you walk through James Bay dozens of renovations, in heritage style, that indicate owners want their houses to appear as they did when they were built. Many are equally proud of their gardens; it's not unusual to spy an English country garden or a perennial bed in the narrow front yards: the blazing annuals and straight-edged flower beds once popular have been replaced by more sprawling arrangements.

Emily Carr House, on the right at 207 Government, is a B.C. government heritage property. Built in 1864, Emily's birthplace in

The Emily Carr House on Government Street.

1871, it is surrounded by a mid-Victorian garden. It's open daily from mid-May to mid-October; at other times of the year, you can still contemplate the fates that brought Richard Carr from England to San Francisco to Victoria, and Emily from dutiful Victorian daughter to writer, rebel and one of Canada's best-known artists.

➤ Opposite the James Bay Inn, turn right on a short pedestrian walkway that leads you to Avalon Road.

The cluster of houses here on Avalon Road, and on Huntington, just around the corner, is the largest group of designated heritage houses in James Bay. Built mostly around 1890, they abound in gingerbread and Italianate details. Take a look at 613, 614, 619, 623, 624 and 634 Avalon.

➤ Take the first left onto Huntington.

Note 310 and 314 Huntington, which have both been beautifully restored.

➤ Turn left on Toronto Street.

At the corner of Government and Toronto is the James Bay Inn, a hotel since 1911 when it was built with "ample space between it and the surrounding property to secure light and fresh air in unlimited quantity." For a number of years, this was the Colonial Hotel, since the

A heritage house on Huntington Place.

owner at the time thought it misleading to call a hotel with no view the James Bay Inn. But history prevailed over strict veracity, and it's been the JBI again for a quarter century. Though it's been overshadowed by newer, grander James Bay hotels, it still provides a stopping place for lunch or a beer.

➤ Follow Toronto past a number of late 19th- and early 20th-century houses (588 and 589 Toronto are both particularly nice) to the five-corners intersection where Toronto, Simcoe and Menzies streets all meet.

James Bay's commercial village meets the needs of James Bayites admirably: grocery store, liquor store, coffee/book/internet café, hairdressers, a place to buy a motorized or four-wheel walker, a place to buy fish and chips, a place to buy flowers, several places— grand to unassuming—to have a coffee or a meal. Trek down below in James Bay Square to the second-hand store, which stocks all those kitchen utensils you can't find in department stores anymore. It's probably unique among second-hand stores: you can take your purchase home for a trial 24 hours, return it if it doesn't suit. The coffee shop across Simcoe Street comes recommended for soup and sandwiches.

➤ Head north on Menzies Street, away from the water, towards the Parliament Buildings. Turn right on Michigan Street.

The shingle-style, frame James Bay United Church, just down from the corner, has been recently restored, painted the seemingly unchurch-like colours of pumpkin and maroon. These are the original colours from 1891. The first attempt to repaint took place in fall; only one wall was completed, and that in the wrong colours— lipstick red and strong orange. The minister received a call shortly after, telling him that the colours of the spirit were white, blue and green; what appeared on the church were the colours of the devil.

Come spring, the entire church was repainted in the proper shades— though not in green, white or blue. The modern stained-glass windows in the church were created in memory of their parents by a family of parishioners who ran a stained-glass business.

Across Michigan, you can see the Michigan Street community garden with its display of xeriscaping—a type of gardening using plants that require less water.

Windows at James Bay United Church.

➤ Return to Menzies and continue north.

If you bought fish and chips or a donair in the village, there's a park across the street here where you can munch and meander, watching the locals at play. In the park is a small two-dimensional labyrinth set out in white stone paths. If you're with the Zen of it all, you can walk the paths and contemplate; if not, you'll probably wonder why anyone bothered. Farther up Menzies is the James Bay Tea Room, an olde English emporium with scones, steak and kidney pie and many varieties of tea.

Take a look at the carriage house on the northeast corner of Superior and Menzies. The Menzies Street Drill Hall at 431 Menzies, built in 1892, contained armouries, a gun shed, officers' and orderlies' rooms and a quartermaster's store. Replaced by the Bay Street Armoury in 1915, the old drill hall serves as government offices.

➤ Turn right into a laneway that is opposite Kingston Street on your left.

This lane leads you behind the drill hall and then the Parliament Buildings, with views of these stone edifices that are different from those usually seen on postcards.

➤ Keep right at the end of the drill hall, then keep left to make your way along the back of the buildings.

The smallpox epidemic of 1892 lowered the boom on Victoria's economic prosperity, so the government decided to help the city out with new parliament buildings. Francis Mawson Rattenbury, a 25-year-old Yorkshireman who had just arrived in Victoria and whose architectural design and unconventional marital life would keep Victoria buzzing for another three decades, won the design competition, presenting plans for three wings that met under a central dome 13 metres (43 feet) in diameter. The central block housed the legislature, flanking blocks of government departments. The buildings, British Columbia stone and slate, were first illuminated in 1897 for Queen Victoria's diamond jubilee; they were officially opened in 1898. The south wing, housing the provincial library, was added in about 1915. Rattenbury met his fate in England, when his young second wife was implicated in his murder, committed by the wife's chauffeur-lover.

Look right: the centennial fountain was built in 1958, to commemorate the founding of the colony of British Columbia in 1858. The raven represents Vancouver Island, the eagle the Queen Charlotte Islands, the bear mainland British Columbia, and the wolf the northern territory of Stickeen (Stikine).

Look up: the rounded south wing houses the provincial library; in niches along it are 14 statues of men important in B.C. history, from Nuu-chah-nulth chief Maquinna to explorer David Thompson to politician Anthony Musgrave. A plaque near the fountain identifies the sculptures. Below the niches in which the sculptures stand are medallions representing Homer, Dante, Shakespeare, Sophocles and Milton, whose books may or may not be in the library that they adorn.

Look even higher up: finally, some women. Around the parapet on the building's dome are 12 female figures chosen from mythology, representing the arts of painting, music, sculpture and archaeology. Captain George Vancouver, explorer and mapper of the B.C. coast, gets the top of the dome all to himself.

➤ Follow along to the end of the main block, then cut left, up and down a set of stone steps through the archway that connects one wing of the buildings to the next. Emerge onto the front lawn of the Parliament Buildings, and turn left.

On the front lawn you can find a number of commemorative trees and statues: a giant sequoia planted in about 1863, a red cedar planted in 1988 when that tree was adopted as the province's official

Statues in their niches at the back of the Parliament Buildings.

tree, a memorial to governor Sir James Douglas, a war memorial, a statue of Queen Victoria, a totem pole and yet another fountain.

➤ At the end of the buildings, bear right with the walkway towards the Inner Harbour and Belleville Street.

Across Menzies is yet another commemorative fountain, this one bearing the emblems of the provinces and marking Canadian Confederation.

➤ Turn left on Belleville Street.

Across Belleville is the former CPR steamship terminal, born in a day when the water route between Victoria, Vancouver and Seattle was thronged with ships. If you're in the mood, cross Belleville and find the symbols of the sea Rattenbury incorporated into a creation that he envisioned as a temple of Neptune.

A block along Belleville is a collection of buildings now given the name of Belleville Park. This was the city's first ritzy district, with its fine view across the harbour and separation from the actual commercial goings-on downtown. The Alexander Gray House at 321 Belleville is one of the nicest, pleasantly austere, without the frills and furbelows of some of the more ostentatious mansions up the street. Gray's drygoods company didn't do that well, and he had to take paid employment and sell his Belleville Street house. The next owner was George Jackson, a successful tailor who decided to become a doctor, went to medical school, then produced a breakfast food that made him his fortune.

Next door, built in 1895, is Loretto Hall, now known—and who can tell what either name has to do with Victoria?—as the Gatsby Mansion. William and Amelia Pendray copied a San Francisco style they had admired on their honeymoon; the garden, with its sculpted bushes, reflects William's love of topiary. Pendray was as good at making money as his neighbour, Jackson. He realized soon after arriving in Victoria in 1875 that well-off Victorians threw out kitchen fat and tallow, then paid high prices for imported soap. His British Columbia Soap Works thrived, thus proving his contention that "if people are ever to become contented, happy and prosperous, they must first be made clean." He was equally successful in other industries. But his personal life was less happy: one son was killed almost outside the front door when a horse bolted. In 1913, Pendray was killed when part of a fire sprinkling system in his factory fell on him.

In tourist season, craftspeople sell their wares at an artisans' lane behind the buildings.

> ➤ Where the ferry terminal parking lot ends and Belleville curves left to become Pendray Street, cross to the water side of the street and bear right onto the pedestrian walkway. The walkway forks; stay on the right-hand fork, heading towards the water.

Walk through Centennial Park, a rather forgotten tribute to B.C.'s entry into Confederation.

> ➤ Go down the steps at the far side of the small park, to the waterfront walkway. Turn left.

This walkway flanks Laurel Point, an industrial and wharf area for decades, but now redeveloped into hotels, condominiums and green space.

As you walk along, you'll see a small cannon on your right. Interestingly, given it was financed partly by Delta Hotels, owners of the Laurel Point Inn, it is aimed, not at potential invaders arriving by sea, but at potential hotel rivals across the Inner Harbour. Ahead on the left is a pavilion that celebrates Victoria's relationship with Morioka, its sister city in Japan, presented on the fifth anniversary of the twinning of the cities.

Farther on, the walkway is flanked by condominiums that give rise to lifestyle envy: these must be the only apartments in Victoria guarded by a moat, with a waterfall, pots of plants, a marina and a magnificent view in front.

➤ Just before the Coast Harbourside Hotel (sign for Blue Crab Restaurant), turn left on a path that leads you up stairs and to the street. (If you miss this path, turn left when the waterfront walkway ends, and head—cautiously—up the hotel driveway.)
Turn right at the street (Kingston). Continue past a three-way stop sign, then turn right into Fisherman's Wharf.

Officially known as the Erie Street floats, Fisherman's Wharf has been under threat for several decades as harbour officials think about turfing out (waving out?) the houseboats and few remaining fishing boats that, presumably, don't generate enough revenue to satisfy the management. Until they succeed, however, you can still buy live crab when the crab boat is docked, consider whether you could live in a small floating space rocked by the waves, or munch fish and

One of the denizens surveys his domain at Fisherman's Wharf.

chips from Barb's Place, a Victoria institution (if you're there between March 1 and the end of October). Some have even been known to bring along something drinkable in a brown paper bag, and go and sit on the playing field above the floats. After all, how can you eat fish and chips without drinking beer?

➤ Turn left on the driveway that leads out of the wharf area, just before a new condominium development (it's opposite Dock 5). Continue straight ahead onto Dallas Road.

Shoal Point at 21 Dallas, a new condominium development, boasts of a lifestyle that includes private greenhouses, a concierge and original prices between $250,000 and $1.75 million. Take a look and decide whether you agree with the Urban Development Institute (tied for best high-rise, multi-family development in B.C. in 2000) or *Monday Magazine* ("unequivocally...the ugliest monument to atrocious planning on the Inner Harbour").

➤ Continue along Dallas Road.

The coast guard station is first up on the right, marked by two retired buoys once used to identify channels in treacherous waters. The conical red buoy dates to 1896. The larger green buoy with a light on top is also of an outmoded type.

The unpaved parking lot, boat launch and small building on the right have allowed community access to the water for decades. The James Bay Anglers Association charges a minimum fee for members, who can launch their boats here, one of the few easily accessible, inexpensive launch sites on the harbour. But Transport Canada's new money-making mandate was set to doom the JBA: the new market lease value was $14,000 a year, a stiff fee for the 250 mostly older club members who like to put their rowboats and small motorboats into the water here for a day's fishing. After much publicity and discussion, TC agreed to drop the fee to a much more affordable figure, and to pay the club for the upkeep of the property.

best places
to drink coffee while people-watching:

This isn't about the coffee. Some like it strong, some like it weak. Some want organic, some just don't care. But for ambience and people-watching, try the following, in no particular order:

QVs, Chinatown, corner of Fisgard and Government. Sit outdoors and watch the nightlife in Chinatown, not to mention the street life heading up from under the Johnson Street Bridge. Tour 1.

Olive Olios, Cadboro Bay Village. Sit outside on a stone bench behind the lovely perennial garden and watch the tennis players and dog walkers. Tour 7.

Moka House, Cook Street Village, Fairfield. You might be in a hurry or a Starbucks fan, in which case, you can go across the street. But Cook Street's laid-back crowd hangs out here. Tour 4.

James Bay Coffee, Books and Internet Café, in James Bay Village. Limited outdoor seating on the sidewalk, but you can snaffle a window table and a book to read. Tour 2.

Torrefazione Italia, 1234 Government Street. You have to be super-cool to have coffee here. Tour 1.

All along the water here are Victoria's deep-sea wharves, built when it became clear that the Inner Harbour could not accommodate such prestigious ships as the *Empress of India,* steaming across the Pacific on the silk route. The mayor of the time was wounded by the fact that such a ship must anchor offshore; it made Victoria look, well, not world-class. So he went to work to make sure wharves were constructed that could accept the largest and deepest-draught of the world's ships.

On the right are a helijet pad and the Ogden Point docks, once home to a cold storage fish plant and a grain elevator, now the docks for cruise ships—always interesting arrivals that are met by a curious combination of new taxis and old horse-drawn carriages.

At the end of the docks, the breakwater angles out across the water. The 800-metre-long (half-mile) pier breaks the force of the strong southeasterlies that would otherwise batter the wharves. It was built in 1919 of concrete and granite slabs. Today, it's a place for Victorians to walk or run. Fishers cast out from the rocks at its base and scuba divers slip into the water on its east side.

For years, the hardest thing to find in the city was a café with a view. That's changed now, with half a dozen looking out over the water. Among them is the Ogden Point Café, where you can stop for a coffee or a bite to eat while watching the waves slap against the breakwater. Take note of the native plants along the pathway to the café.

➤ Continue along Dallas Road to the starting point of the tour.

Scuba divers prepare to submerge along Dallas Road near the breakwater.

VICTORIA WEST / SELKIRK WATER

WHAT YOU'LL FIND:

Harbour walkways, waterfront pubs, ships in for refits, pocket parks.

BACKGROUND:

For many years, Victoria West was the industrial part of central Victoria, home to wharves, waterfront industry and some of the city's less prosperous residential areas. When real estate agents said that "location, location, location" was the most important part of any real estate deal, Vic West was close to the bottom of their list. If you wanted waterfront property, this was probably the place to find it cheapest.

The development of the Songhees area just across the bridge from downtown changed that image. From native villages to industrial development to luxury hotel and expensive condominiums is a bit of a leap—especially when there isn't a mature tree in sight and the condos aren't everyone's idea of good design. But everyone agrees that the view from the waterfront walkway is one of the best in town, and the walk itself one of the most pleasant. The rest of Vic West is getting something of a refit as well, with heritage houses being renovated and a new shopping centre in service.

With the extension of the Galloping Goose Trail, walkers can now follow the shores of the part of the Gorge waterway known as Selkirk Water, completing the two long sides of the Vic West triangle on walking paths, with just a short base that crosses from harbour to Gorge on streets and paths.

WATCH FOR:

Twisted arbutus, power walkers, competitive rowers, buff runners (no, not in the buff), plastic shrouds on still-leaky condos.

TIMING:

About a two-hour walk at a reasonable pace; half a day if you stop for breakfast, a glass of wine, lunch or a picnic. Fairly flat, but with some minor ups and downs along the way.

TO REACH THE ROUTE:

This is a circle tour, so it can be joined anywhere en route. Tour notes begin at the west end of the Johnson Street Bridge, on

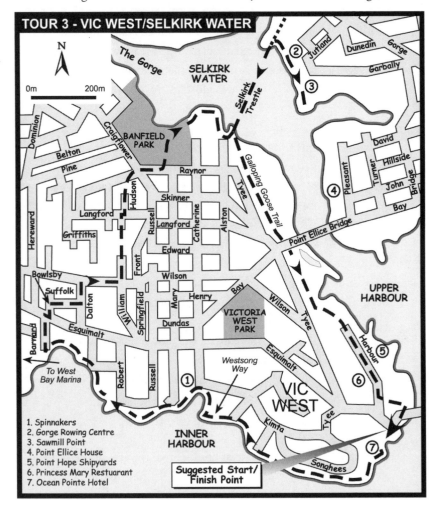

TOUR 3 - VIC WEST/SELKIRK WATER

N

0m   200m

The Gorge

SELKIRK WATER

Selkirk Trestle

Jutland

Dunedin

Gorge

Garbally

David

Hillside

BANFIELD PARK

Craigflower

Dominion

Belton

Pine

Raynor

Galloping Goose Trail

Tyee

Pleasant

Turner

John

Bridge

Hudson

Skinner

Catherine

Alston

Bay

Hereward

Langford

Russell

Langford

Point Ellice Bridge

Griffiths

Front

Edward

Bowlsby

Wilson

Suffolk

Dalton

Mary

Henry

Bay

Wilson

UPPER HARBOUR

William

Springfield

Dundas

VICTORIA WEST PARK

Tyee

Barnard

Esquimalt

Esquimalt

Harbour

Robert

Russell

Westsong Way

VIC WEST

To West Bay Marina

INNER HARBOUR

Kimta

Tyee

1. Spinnakers
2. Gorge Rowing Centre
3. Sawmill Point
4. Point Ellice House
5. Point Hope Shipyards
6. Princess Mary Restuarant
7. Ocean Pointe Hotel

Songhees

Suggested Start/
Finish Point

Westsong Way. Most of the parking along the way, on the Songhees development and at Selkirk Water, is limited to two hours during the day, Monday through Saturday. Two small parking areas off Songhees Road offer three-and-a-half-hour parking; there is some three-hour parking available at the end of Robert or Russell streets off Esquimalt Road. Otherwise, you might want to park on Kimta Road off Catherine Street, or at Selkirk Water, and do your pubbing or grubbing when you have finished your walk. Bus #25 Munro or #6 Esquimalt will take you to the tour starting point, or you can walk the short distance from downtown across the Johnson Street Bridge. Bus #8 Finlayson (to Camosun Interurban) or #10 Gorge will take you to the intersection of Gorge and Jutland; from this corner it's just a block or so to the Selkirk Water waterfront.

For a change: when the little harbour ferries are bustling about (call 708-0201 for information; the ferries run spring, summer and fall), you can walk Westsong to its end at West Bay, catch a ferry across the harbour to Laurel Point, then circle back along the water through downtown to Westsong. See tours 1 and 2 for more details of this walk.

THE ROUTE:

➤   Begin at the west end of the Johnson Street Bridge, facing away from downtown, towards the open end of the harbour, with the water on your left. Westsong Way begins here. Follow Westsong Way along the water.

The Johnson Street Bridge behind you is a lift span, counter-balanced by a weight at one end of the bridge. A bleating horn signals to pedestrians and motorists that the span is about to lift, to allow a boat to enter the upper harbour. Those who hear the horn in time turn tail and head for the Bay Street Bridge; all others wait in line for the slow-moving marine traffic.

This section of Westsong Way opened in 1990, part of the walkway that now follows most of the shore of the harbour from West Bay to past Laurel Point. For the first kilometre (.6 mile), Westsong borders the Songhees condominium developments, where residents have some of the best views in Victoria.

On your left, not far from the beginning of the walkway, a cluster of rocky outcroppings is the backdrop for what may once have been the world's tallest totem pole. Since the pole had artificial supports, still visible, many considered it a bit of a phoney. That discussion is moot now that the pole has been severely cropped—it was considered a navigation hazard for the float planes that fly into the harbour and a possible danger in high winds. Near the pole are four concrete platforms that were once the foundation for a water tower.

The rocks form a natural viewpoint over the harbour, where you can see kayaks glide by, float planes taxi to and from their docks on the harbourfront, and the last remaining passenger ship to dock in the harbour. The m.v. *Coho*, sailing between Victoria and Port Angeles on the American shore, is the inheritor of a long tradition that saw steamships ply between Victoria, Seattle and Victoria, with other runs up the coasts of Vancouver Island. Look back across the harbour to see old town. Across from the Songhees are the Parliament Buildings and Laurel Point. In the distance, on the Songhees side of the harbour, are the last remaining

Dolphins and a girl having a good time along Westsong Way. (Anton Studios)

Looking back at the old town from Westsong Way. (Anton Studios)

oil-tank farm on the harbour and the military buildings at Work Point, part of the Department of National Defence establishment in Esquimalt.

➤ Keep left along the water.

Along the way on your right, you'll see a statue entitled *Victoria Pacifica*, dolphins and a swimmer by sculptor John Barney Weaver, flanked by two bronzes of nude women, also by Weaver.

➤ Past the end of Paul Kane Place (distance and route sign on your right), keep right up the slope towards the road. Keep left at the road, then turn left again along the walkway to return to the waterfront.

The building on the right houses Spinnakers, Victoria's first brew pub, opened in 1984. Back in those dark ages, it was hard to find a waterfront pub anywhere in the region and impossible to quaff a natural brew. Spinnakers changed all that, starting with the Extra

Special Bitter that the brewmaster still produces. Stop by before the tour for breakfast, after for a beer. The view from the outside patio and balconies is great.

> ➤ Continue along the waterfront walkway.

The walkway has a devoted following, with many people taking a daily stroll along the water. In this section, the attractions are mainly natural: birds that winter in these waters, among them herons, kingfishers and a fair variety of ducks and gulls, as well as black cormorants, ungainly on land, poetry in the air or in the water. Arbutus trees curve across the walkway, and smaller native plants, plus shrub roses, lavender and winter-flowering rosemary border the path. Keep an eye out for a cove where a pole with nesting boxes attached rises from the water. The boxes are for purple martins, a relatively rare nester in the area. These swallows, named for the dark purplish male, traditionally nested in old pilings; the boxes protect them from voracious starlings.

(The next instructions take you from the walkway across Vic West to the Gorge. If you want to extend your walk along the harbour, you can continue another 600 metres/ 660 yards to the West Bay Marina, a distance of 2.7 kilometres/1.7 miles from the Johnson Street Bridge. Then retrace your steps to rejoin the tour route as noted below.)

Arbutus trees cast shadows on walkway and grass. (Anton Studios)

➤ Past a gazebo on your left and white apartment building on your right, turn right on Barnard Street (no sign, but it leads past some tennis courts in a small park). Cross Esquimalt Road at the crosswalk you see to your left (traffic roars through here, so the crosswalk is a better bet than crossing at the nearest corner), then return to Bowlsby Place and turn left (away from the water). Bowlsby curves into Suffolk Street. Turn left at the stop sign onto Dalton. Turn right at the next street, which is Wilson. Cross Wilson at the crosswalk just beyond the railway tracks, at William Street.
Follow William Street into the dead-end lane in front of you, to a pathway that goes between playing fields and Victoria West School. This path emerges through a park onto Langford Street. Just to your right and ahead is Hudson Street. Follow Hudson to its end.

This narrow lane is flanked by interesting houses—not heritage-designated, but full of character nonetheless.

➤ At the end of Hudson, turn right on a path just past a chain-link fence. Follow the path through the small park, then turn right on the street at its end (Raynor). Cross Craigflower Road ahead. Walk past the tennis courts on your left and turn left on the pathway. Continue down to the waterfront and turn right on the trail.

The houses above this trail date back to the time when life along the Gorge Waterway attracted a number of well-off residents who built relatively modest but very attractive waterfront or waterview houses. To the right above the water just before the Selkirk Trestle are a cluster of these houses, on Arthur Currie Lane.

➤ Turn left from the trail onto the Selkirk Trestle, and cross Selkirk Water.

This 300-metre-long (1,000-foot) fir and hemlock trestle used to inspire fear in those who crossed it while it was still a railway bridge: no railings, one or two stepouts in case a train came by, moving water visible straight down between the ties. When the mills that used to operate on the south side of the water closed, the trains ran no more and the trestle deteriorated. A 1995 fire badly damaged the bridge; fortunately, money was found to restore it as a vital link in the 60-kilometre (37-mile) Galloping Goose Trail, an urban, suburban and rural route that goes from the Johnson Street Bridge along abandoned railway grades to Sidney and Sooke. Now, several thousand people cross the trestle every day, walking, cycling, scootering, rollerblading, some for enjoyment or exercise, some as part of their daily commute to work. Look down to see the silver flash of minnows in the water, a crab scuttling along the bottom and other signs that the cleaning up of the Gorge has been successful.

➤ At the end of the trestle, continue along the trail to the first underpass.

Year-round, walkers, runners, cyclists and skateboarders use the Selkirk Trestle, once a railway bridge across the water.

This path follows Cecilia Creek, one of the many streams that used to drain into the Gorge. Cecilia Creek is being renewed, with the hope that salmon will once more spawn here. A hundred metres or so (330 feet) along the trail, painted on the concrete tunnel that runs under Gorge Road, is the Burnside-Gorge community mural by artist Frank Lewis. It's remarkable on several counts: for the artistic talent displayed, for the sheer physical effort it must have required, and for the fact that graffiti artists have left it strictly alone.

> ➤ Return back to the beginning of the trestle and turn left along the waterfront.

Note on your left a huge checkerboard; try recruiting enough people to play checkers. Birdhouses along the water are intended, as are the ones along Westsong, for purple martins.

The redevelopment of this former industrial site into a residential/commercial/office conglomerate has won awards for its architects. The architecture isn't to everyone's taste, but there's no denying that the area is gradually coming alive, especially on days when scullers and other rowers put their oars into the water at the Gorge Rowing Centre.

Competitive rowing has been a tradition on the Gorge from the 1890s. From the 1920s to the 1950s, no summer was complete without competitive regattas that pitted Victoria's best against those from throughout the Pacific northwest. Rowing moved to Elk Lake in the 1950s, returning to the Gorge for the Head of the Gorge regatta each autumn in the 1970s. In 1996, the Gorge Rowing Centre opened here, bringing hundreds of competitive and recreational rowers to the waterway for classes from beginner to advanced, in singles, doubles, quads and eights, as well as for a dragon boat program that culminates with a dragon boat race each August.

Sawmill Point, just beyond the rowing centre, houses a chiropractor specializing in sports injuries, a fitness gym and several other businesses. Take a moment to look at the architecture and

bEST plACES
to have a picnic lunch:

The beach at **Cadboro Bay.** Tour 7.

Westsong Way, in spring or autumn. Tour 3.

Beacon Hill Park. Tour 4.

WORST plACE
to have a picnic lunch:

Westsong Way in summer, when the rotting seaweed sends out its siren smell. Tour 3.

---

offices here, and praise yourself for partaking of such a healthy activity as walking. Several coffee shops and restaurants can be found a street or so back from the water. At the end of the development, take a look across the small bay to see some of the last remaining industrial activity along the Gorge: you can watch cranes and trucks manoeuvre ex-cars and ex-trucks from scrap pile to barge.

➤ Return to the trestle, and recross Selkirk Water. Turn left at the end of the trestle to follow the trail along the waterfront.

A pavilion and plaques just to your right here list the names of contributors to the Cross-Canada Trail that spans the nation. It begins here, in Victoria, and ends in St. John's, Newfoundland.

This part of the Galloping Goose Trail traces the shore of Selkirk Water and the Upper Harbour as far as the Johnson Street Bridge, where it joins up with the Westsong Walkway.

To the left, across the water, you can catch sight of a small dock, the landing stage for Point Ellice House, the last remaining of the fine houses that once stood along the shores of Selkirk Water. Now a provincial heritage site, it was built in 1861 for gold commissioner and judge Peter O'Reilly and his family.

Follow the trail under the Point Ellice Bridge, more frequently referred to as the Bay Street Bridge. Bridge abutments here have not been ignored by the spray-paint brigade, and there are often signs that someone is camping out in the dry and somewhat warm. Though the bridge is solid now, a century ago it was the scene of one of Victoria's greatest tragedies. On May 26, 1896, it collapsed under the weight of a streetcar carrying 140 passengers, 80 more than its intended capacity. Fifty-five people died that day; another 27 were badly injured.

Past the bridge, the Gorge opens into the upper harbour, once a bustling industrial area, now slowly being gentrified. On your right as you emerge from under the bridge is a piece of wasteland much loved by young mountain bikers, who climb and somersault along its dirt hills.

The trail leads onto Harbour Road, which has a lane set apart for walkers. The Point Hope Shipyards are the last of the working shipyards that once surrounded the upper harbour. From the entrance, you can see cranes, pots of marine paint, various chandlery and all the paraphernalia that goes along with refitting ships. On the right along Harbour Road is the Princess Mary restaurant, a

A fisherman who has arrived here by bicycle throws a crab pot into the water near the Bay Street Bridge.

long-time favourite among long-time Victorians. There's a green bandsaw from an old mill beside the road on the left, a home for the reproduction of classic Whitehall dories on the right. Almost at the end of the strip are the headquarters of the Sail and Life Training association, a Christian-oriented group that provides young people with experience aboard the society's classic sailing ships. The society has built a number of sailing ships; its first, the Grand Banks schooner, *Robertson II*, has been retired and should be visible at the heritage shipyard here, where it serves as a classroom.

➤ Follow the path up and across the rail line, above Johnson Street. At the small signpost, follow the arrow that points towards downtown, behind the Ocean Pointe Hotel. Turn right on the second path, just before you go onto the bridge, between Japanese-looking wooden structures, continuing between the hotel and the waterfront to return to the tour starting point.

Vessels at the shipyards along Harbour Road form a foreground for old Victoria buildings.

BEACON HILL / FAIRFIELD

WHAT YOU'LL FIND:

Trees, flowers, pathways and ponds; coffee and fish and chips and pubs; heritage houses and graveyard stories; waves and waterfront and magnificent ocean views.

BACKGROUND:

Beacon Hill is Victoria's largest and oldest urban park, 74 hectares (185 acres) of relatively wild Garry oak meadow and neatly manicured flower beds set aside as parkland in the 1850s by prescient Hudson's Bay Company man and colonial governor-to-be James Douglas. Somehow, the park manages to encompass a wide variety of activities, from those that go on in Lovers' Lane to charity walks to musical concerts to contemplation undertaken in relative solitude. Recent lawsuits have made it clear, though, that there's an equally wide understanding of what this park should be: from as undisturbed and natural as possible (though it's a little late for that) to the home of various commercial ventures. Looks like the gavel will come down on the side of as little commercial activity as possible, while retaining the possibility of the charity walks and other non-profit events.

The park is bordered by the oceanfront to the south and the district of Fairfield to the east. Fairfield the funky, some might say, since residences vary from small and elderly apartments to restored historic houses, and residents from young and gay, to elderly and determined, to dead. The first two meet in Cook Street Village, another of Victoria's attractive commercial centres. The last have been gathered in Ross Bay Cemetery, where, in another era, storm-driven waves rolled in and then back out, carrying with them the coffins and bones of some of those relegated to the less favoured parts of the graveyard.

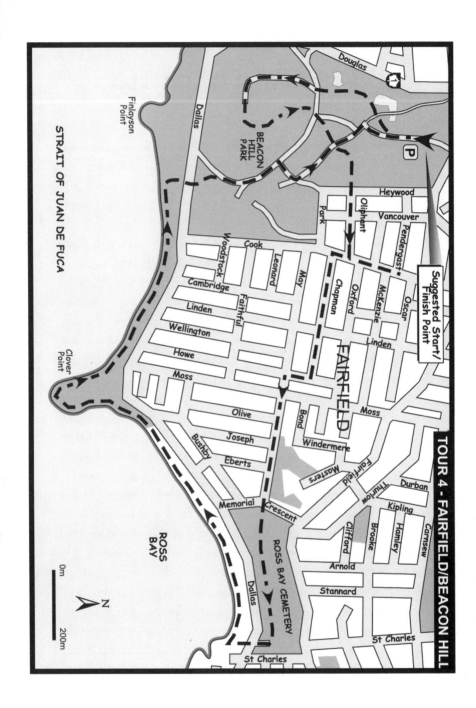

STRAIT OF JUAN DE FUCA

Finlayson Point

Clover Point

BEACON HILL PARK

Dallas

Douglas

Heywood

Park

Oliphant

Vancouver

Pendergast

Oscar

McKenzie

Oxford

Linden

FAIRFIELD

Cook

Woodstock

Leonard

May

Chapman

Cambridge

Fairthful

Linden

Wellington

Howe

Moss

Moss

Olive

Bond

Joseph

Windermere

Bushby

Eberts

Masters

Fairfield

Thurlow

Durban

Memorial

Crescent

Kipling

Hamley

Carnsew

ROSS BAY

Clifford

Brooke

Dallas

ROSS BAY CEMETERY

Arnold

Stannard

St Charles

St Charles

Suggested Start/ Finish Point

TOUR 4 - FAIRFIELD/BEACON HILL

0m   200m

N

If you're interested in specific graves, check the Old Cemeteries web site (www.oldcem.bc.ca/) for maps and details before you go walking.

WATCH FOR:

Kite-flyers, windsurfers, dog owners, children playing, Sunday-morning coffee drinkers, tombstone aficionados.

TIMING:

The route covers seven or eight kilometres (about five miles) of flat walking, two hours at a stroll, half a day if you choose to stop for food or drink, gawking at the view or reading the inscriptions on tombstones.

TO REACH THE ROUTE:

This circular walk can be joined anywhere en route. To begin as shown below, follow Quadra Street south to its end at Southgate, cross Southgate and enter Beacon Hill Park via Arbutus Way. You can park for 3½ hours beside the road, or continue on to the first parking lot on the left. You can also park elsewhere in the park, or along Dallas Road, and pick up the route from there. Parking elsewhere on the route is time-limited, or restricted to residents. Bus #5 Beacon Hill or #11 Beacon Hill will drop you at the edge of Beacon Hill Park, or you can make the short walk from downtown.

THE ROUTE:

➤ Begin at the parking lot beside Arbutus Way, across Southgate from the south end of Quadra Street.

Arbutus and Garry oaks, the two species that are the signature trees of southern Vancouver Island, are found throughout the park. Perhaps most noticeable are the row of arbutus along Arbutus Way and the Garry oaks in the meadow beside the road. Arbutus trees, known elsewhere as Pacific madrone, are characterized by their leathery evergreen leaves, peeling red bark and the shiny limbs below that bark. Garry oaks spread their characteristic gnarled and twisted branches across a winter sky. Their furrowed grey bark is equally picturesque.

➤ From the parking lot, cross the road to Goodacre Lake (there's a large signpost halfway down the south side of the lake).
Follow the pathway along the left side of the lake, then bear right up the steps. Take a stroll over the stone bridge to your right, then return across the bridge and continue straight on.

Goodacre Lake is named for Lawrence Goodacre, butcher, chairman of the parks committee and city councillor, who supplied free meat for the animals in the park zoo three times a week from 1890 to 1907. The zoo was gradually phased out; now only a petting farm remains of the previous animal attractions. The stone bridge was built in 1889 to resemble a rustic medieval bridge.

In late spring, fields of blue camas spread across the park's Garry oak meadows.

Waterfowl and seagulls crowd the park, especially in winter, when they find visitors dispensing bags of day-old bread despite signs that plead with people not to do so. Legions of Canada geese, in particular, have become a problem here as in other south Island and Lower Mainland parks; their ability to consume grass and almost anything else in their way and drop copious guano makes them unpopular guests. But many a small child is enthralled by the ducks that waddle over to see what's on offer, and the group is duly photographed for Grandma's album.

➤ Returning from the bridge, keep right at the smaller paved path (there's a "No Cycling" sign at the start of this path). Where the path splits, keep left, through a grove of cedars and past a green building on the left.
At a Y in the path, keep right, then left to Fountain Lake— which contains, reasonably enough, a fountain, as well as ducks and aquatic plants.
Keep left at the Y at the end of the lake, and continue to the park's main road, Circle Drive. Cross Circle Drive at the crosswalk and follow the road ahead up to the top of Beacon Hill.

Two beacons were placed here in the 1840s, to help mariners locate the underwater hazard of Brotchie Ledge. One was topped with a triangle, one with a square target or drum. "When the observer saw the latter through the triangle," notes a history of the park, "he was on the rock." Seems a little late to realize that.

From Beacon Hill, the Strait of Juan de Fuca is visible north and south, with the Olympic Mountains beyond the strait.

➤ To return back down the hill, find the path that heads down just past the green building and flagpole. Follow it along a metal fence past the Petting Farm back to Circle Drive. Recross the road at the crosswalk.

Take a look just to your left at the most inviting climbing tree in Victoria. This giant sequoia has attracted generations of young park visitors. Towards the front of the putting green on your left is a memorial to "Scotland's Immortal Bard," Robbie Burns, donated to the city in 1900.

➤ Follow the path that leads to a lake ahead.

Continue straight on past the lake, which was once named Rose Lake. Now that the rose gardens are in a different place in the park, it has lost its name without gaining another.

➤ Turn left into the sundial garden, then right to a park road which has public toilets just on the other side.

The sundial was placed in the garden in 1947, the same year that the first power mower was purchased for the park, something that must have come as a great relief to the gardeners. They don't have as much mowing to do as might be thought, however: the grass in the meadows is left to grow until the camas and other spring-flowering bulbs have completed their cycle, a month or two after most Victoria gardeners have hauled their own mowers out of the garage for their first assault on the lawn.

➤ Cross the road and turn left. Keep right past the fountain on your right, and continue to the right, past a children's playground.

Just before you leave Beacon Hill, you could consider the exhortation in the *British Colonist* of June 7, 1861, which seems to suggest that daily stress is not an invention of modern life: "We are in favour of everybody semi-occasionally taking a ride or walk through Beacon Hill Park, either to inhale the sea breeze, admire the scenery, view the flowers and enjoy their aroma, listen to the warbling of the songsters of the forest, strengthen their muscles, fill their lungs with pure oxygen, walk or trot, gallop or run, or spread themselves

Walkers take a break at a coffee house in Cook Street Village.

gypsy-like and have a real sense of the extension of human liberty and the blessings of semi-occasionally don't care-a-rap-ativeness." As long, of course, as it's only semi-occasionally.

➤ Keep right again on a paved path, bear left at a Y in the path, and follow it out across the field ahead to Heywood Avenue. Cross Heywood and continue ahead on Oliphant Avenue. Follow Oliphant two blocks to Cook Street. Turn left to explore Cook Street Village.

Like Victoria's other small commercial villages that serve distinct residential areas, Cook Street Village has a charm severely lacking in malls and superstores. In the village are a fish-and-chip shop, several restaurants, several coffee houses, two grocery stores, a garden store, a pub and a variety of other stores worth the browsing. If you're a videophile, stop by Pic-a-Flic to check out their collection of vintage, classic and foreign films, one of the best in the city.

➤ Past Pic-a-Flic, cross the road at the next crosswalk and return back down Cook Street to Chapman Street. Turn left. Follow Chapman to Howe. Turn right.

Along these residential blocks between Beacon Hill Park and the Ross Bay Cemetery, you'll see the mix of housing that is Fairfield: tiny workers' houses and larger, middle-class houses that go back to before World War II, plus a few newer houses in postwar style. Many of the older houses are now being restored; look for tidy paint jobs and renewed front yards, especially along Chapman Street.

➤ Turn left on May Street.

If you didn't get your coffee fix in the Cook Street Village, you can visit the coffee house on Moss Street, near May; try out their daily soup.

➤ Follow May Street to its end at Memorial Crescent.

Along the way, you'll note the outcropping of rock on your left that is a reminder of the underlying rocky structure of the region. Glance into the backyard of Stewart Monumental Works, since 1896 the makers of gravestones and monuments for Victoria's dear departed. You could pick out the style you would prefer for yourself.

At Memorial Crescent, you can take a short detour to the left to see a trio of heritage houses that were built in the 1880s for working-class families.

➤ Cross Memorial Crescent to enter the Ross Bay Cemetery.

You can wander at will through the cemetery. But before you do, you might want to orient yourself: the cemetery forms a long oblong, bounded on this side by Memorial Crescent, on the north by Fairfield Road, on the south by Dallas Road and the waterfront. Eventually, you want to end up at the east end of the cemetery, opposite where you are now, heading for the waterfront.

The cemetery is considered an excellent example of a Victorian romantic cemetery, with trees, walkways and benches for contemplation of eternity. This Victorian ideal required that one look upon nature in a rural setting—and that's what this area was in 1873, when it was chosen as the city's third cemetery. The original central portion of the cemetery was expanded with purchase of the western portion in 1893 (burials began in 1900) and the eastern portion in 1906. The cemetery and bay are named for Isabella Ross, who originally owned the land that today makes up the eastern two-thirds of the graveyard. A fur-trader's wife of European and Ojibwan heritage, she was the first registered female landowner in British Columbia. Isabella's buried here, by the way, unmarked until 1994, when the Old Cemeteries Society erected a handsome but plain stone marker, her grave is near the Dallas Road edge of the cemetery, about a third of the way along from the eastern boundary.

Fairfield's houses are often both historic and modest.

Many of Victoria's (and British Columbia's) 19th-century elite are buried here, among them Judge Matthew Baillie Begbie, early and eccentric premier Amor de Cosmos, goldrusher Billy Barker and James and Amelia Douglas. Also resting here are artist and writer Emily Carr, and the miners' angel, prospector Nellie Cashman, who was a part of almost every North American gold rush from the early 1870s until she died in Victoria in 1925.

If you want to find specific graves, you'll need patience or information from a map of the cemetery (see web site listed above). Otherwise, you can muse upon 19th-century society that dictated that you be buried according to your religion or your race: graves of those of Asian heritage, for example, were located along the insecure seaside edge of the cemetery. Or you can look for examples of the monument-maker's work: a bronze firefighter's helmet, a tiny stone chair with baby booties on it, protecting angels and hovering ravens.

Many of the trees in the cemetery were planted in the 1930s, but a few date much further back. Look for an Atlas cedar with

Ross Bay Cemetery was laid out to encourage thoughtful contemplation of life and its inevitable end.

This gravestone in Ross Bay Cemetery marks a Japanese grave.

47 trunks. Native to the Atlas Mountains of Morocco, the Atlas is a true cedar (*Cedrus*), unlike our common native western red cedar (*Thuja*). Many city trees have their origins in the cemetery: gardeners took cuttings from here to start new trees that were planted along Victoria streets. The windbreak along the seaward edge of the cemetery was planted in the 1930s, established with cuttings taken from the older, salt spray–tolerant trees.

➤ When you reach the east end of the cemetery, turn right (towards the water). Follow this path out of the cemetery to a paved lane. At the end of the lane, a ramp leads down to Dallas Road. Follow the ramp, then cross Dallas Road. Turn right, along the water. Follow the walkway along Ross Bay.

For years, ocean storm waves crashed unimpeded onto the shore here, washing away large sections of the high bank. Stories are told of bones tumbled out of caskets, and caskets swept away to sea. Since most of these graves belonged to Chinese interred here, in 1903 the Chinese Consolidated Benevolent Association established a new Chinese cemetery farther along the waterfront at Harling Point; many of the existing Ross Bay graves were dug up and the coffins relocated to Harling Point. In 1911, a seawall was built to abate the effects of the storms. The seawall kept the waves from the

Testing the winds, a model plane enthusiast prepares for lift-off along the waterfront cliffs. (Anton Studios)

graves, but their fury was still impressive: for decades, Victorians have rushed to Ross Bay whenever the wind and tides thrust high waves over the seawall and onto the road. There was something exhilarating about walking or driving (having evaded the sawhorses set up to block the road) through sea spray, dodging the occasional piece of airborne driftwood. Those same waves, however, were eating away at the waterfront, and in the 1990s, the seawall was rebuilt and water-calming artificial reefs built offshore. Still great when it's stormy here, but not as crazy as it used to be. Now, you'll find fishers standing on the beach casting into the surf, cyclists, joggers, walkers, all sharing the seawall, sidewalk and road.

➤ At the end of Ross Bay, curve left with the wide walkway and walk around Clover Point.

This is one of Victoria's most popular places to sit (in car or out) and watch the waves. Windsurfers zip along on conventional boards or are towed by colourful kites across the city's favourite surfing site, below the Beacon Hill cliffs. Seagulls gather here, screeching into the wind, barely moving aside as a constant procession of cars winds its way around the drive. Look along the Ross Bay side of Clover Point for seals that sometimes poke inquisitive noses above the water; walk along the beach to see ocean plants and creatures in the tidal pools and along the rocks.

James Douglas, founder of Fort Victoria, came ashore near here when he first arrived in 1843. He named the point for the clover he saw spreading across the fields above the cliffs. Between Dallas Road and the waterfront is a marble sculpture entitled *Millennium Peace*, by artist Maarten Schaddelee. Maarten and Nadina Schaddelee donated the sculpture in 2000, to celebrate peace in the new millennium. It depicts an orca and an eagle around a maple leaf that symbolizes Canada.

➤ Return to the waterfront path and continue along the cliffs, past the end of Cook Street on your right. Just before the first thicket of windblown trees and bushes, follow the path to Dallas Road again, and cross at the crosswalk. Enter Beacon Hill Park again via the pathway in front of you.

In late spring, the open spaces and fields to the left are covered with a sweep of the dark blue blooms of camas, officially classed as a bulbous perennial and known for its resemblance to a lily. Some have compared the fields of camas that grew here before the city was established to clear blue lakes that stretched across hill and field. Camas bulbs were dug by the native people of the region for food,

A fisherman tries his luck near Clover Point.

best places
to sit on a bench and contemplate life
(or death):

Anywhere along the **James Bay waterfront.** Tour 2.

Benches near the **Oak Bay Marina.** Tour 6.

Ross Bay Cemetery (really; it's kind of restful). Tour 4.

who cooked them and ate them on their own or used them to sweeten other foods. If you're hungry, beware of white camas, also known as death camas for its highly poisonous nature.

The path will take you past the former site of what was for many years the world's tallest totem pole. It was surpassed by one in Alert Bay, near the north end of Vancouver Island. In 2000, the pole, which had become a safety hazard, was taken down. A cairn still describes the pole.

➤ Follow the path to the park road. Turn right along this road; turn left at the first road. Stay on this road past the rose gardens on your left, the washrooms on your right. Continue onto Arbutus Way and the starting point of the tour.

ROCKLAND

WHAT YOU'LL FIND:

A crenellated castle, fine rose and native plant gardens, views from the toney part of town, stone walls, turn-of-the-century upper-crust architecture.

BACKGROUND:

Isn't it always the way? Just when you think you have a house in the best part of town, all the rich people move somewhere else. James Bay was Victoria's first district for the wealthy, but by the 1880s, they were looking elsewhere. That's when the Rockland area, part of Fairfield Farm, was established as a subdivision. With superb views out over the ocean, large lots—some as big as 3 hectares (7½ acres) —and finely designed homes, Rockland quickly became the place to live.

Though most of the lots that were developed in the next two decades were somewhat smaller, the houses that were built were no less lavish. The area is still dominated by the largest and most lavish of them all, coal baron Robert Dunsmuir's Craigdarroch Castle. Less historic but equally interesting is Government House, the home of the province's lieutenant-governor.

In time, the rich moved on, to Uplands farther east and south. Along the streets and avenues of Rockland, the fine old houses still hold sway, though smaller houses that are more modern and much less opulent have been built where once gardens and lawns surrounded the Victorian mansions. Many of the old houses have been subdivided, into rental or condominium suites.

WATCH FOR:

The Queen. No, seriously, black limousines with VIPs on board, the ghosts of various Dunsmuirs, verandahs, half-timbered upper storeys.

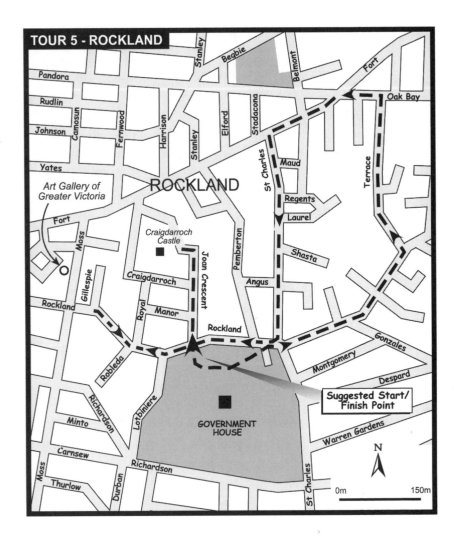

TIMING:

This is a short route, about three kilometres (two miles), with a fair amount of up and down the hills. You can walk it in an hour, or you can spend much of a day if you tour Craigdarroch Castle and spend time in the Government House gardens.

TO REACH THE ROUTE:

This route can be joined at any point. The description begins where Joan Crescent departs from Rockland Avenue. There is some on-street parking here, both east and west of Joan Crescent, plus a few spaces on Joan Crescent itself. Much of the parking between Fort Street and Rockland is time-limited, or reserved for residents. If you plan to spend substantial time at either Craigdarroch Castle or Government House, parking is available there. To reach the route by bus, take #11 Uplands or #14 University from downtown, and walk from Fort Street up Joan Crescent to Craigdarroch Castle.

THE ROUTE:

> ➤ From Rockland Avenue, follow Joan Crescent up the hill and around the curve to Craigdarroch Castle.

The area around Craigdarroch was once the grounds of the castle, 11 terraced hectares (28 acres) of gardens, orchards and oak trees. Long since subdivided, it now contains a combination of period and modern houses, with the occasional condominium building.

Craigdarroch Castle itself is a monument to a man who died before he could move in. Robert Dunsmuir, promoter, coal baron, builder of railways—or, depending on your point of view, suppressor of the working man, indifferent to horrendously unsafe conditions in his mines—was Vancouver Island's most successful capitalist of the 19th century. In 1885, he set in motion his plan to build a castle similar to the baronial castles of his native Scotland. Five years of architectural drawings and construction later, Craigdarroch Castle was the result. With 36 rooms and 35 fireplaces, a 19-metre-long (62-foot) drawing room, fine woodwork, granite columns, frescoes and fine furnishings, at a total cost of half a million dollars, Craigdarroch certainly measured up to the Dunsmuirs' social expectations.

The towers of Craigdarroch Castle rise skyward.

Then fate took a hand: as the family prepared to move in, Robert Dunsmuir died. His widow, Joan, for whom Joan Crescent is named, occupied the house and managed her husband's interests until she died in 1908. Since Dunsmuir's son was building a bigger and better castle for himself out in the countryside west of town, Craigdarroch was sold. Then it was put up for sale again, but no one wanted or could afford such a large house with such great grounds. The land was divided into 144 lots, and each purchaser was given a chance in a draw for the castle itself. The winner couldn't afford his prize; after the mortgagers took over for a mere $35,000, it was used, in turn, as a convalescent home for soldiers, a college, offices and a school of music.

Threatened with demolition in 1959, it was rescued by a major public campaign and has been open to the public as a museum for several decades. Craigdarroch, open every day, hours depending on season, presents a display of life at the turn of the century—or, at least, life as it was lived by those at the very top of Victoria's social pyramid. You can look out the castle's windows at the wretches down below, and consider whether you might not like to take a turn as a baron yourself.

➤ Return to Joan Crescent (turn right as you leave the castle grounds) and follow it back to Rockland Avenue. Turn right and walk west on Rockland.

A number of houses on Rockland west of Joan Crescent are worth a good look: 1346 is an intriguing round stone house; 1321, Ellesmere, was built in 1889, a mock Tudor house for a Scottish merchant; 1322, Schuhuum, is one of the older houses in the area, built in 1894 for Hewitt Bostock, cattleman, journalist and politician. Now known as the Galt House Apartments, the mansion at 1320 was built in 1913 for a department store owner.

A cairn on the corner of Rockland and Gillespie notes Rockland's residential origins. Below the cairn is a time capsule created in the year 2000, to be opened in the year 2100.

➤ Turn back at Gillespie and walk back east along Rockland.

The parade of upmarket houses continues: 1337, Robleda, is a Tudor revival style house, built for capitalist John Arbuthnot in 1906; 1369, Stonyhurst, built in about 1884 and now much altered, was first occupied by an importer and wholesaler; 1385, ca. 1911, was built for a hotelier; and 1393 was built in 1913. Outside 1325 Rockland are several magnificent sequoias; one is more than a metre (over three feet) in diameter, some 25 metres (82 feet) tall. These are coast redwoods, relatively rare in Victoria, since they are not as winterhardy as their cousins, the more common giant sequoias. Known as the world's tallest tree, *Sequoia sempervirens* can grow to a hundred metres (330 feet) in height, 4.5 metres (15 feet) in diameter. Native to California and southern Oregon, they can live to a great age: the most ancient ever found was thought to be 2,200 years old.

Lotbiniere Avenue, a narrow lane leading to your right along the iron and stone wall that contains Government House, was named for the marvellously titled Sir Henry Joly de Lotbiniere, B.C.'s lieutenant-governor around the turn of the century.

> Past Lotbiniere, turn right into the grounds of Government House. The driveway will take you past the entrance to the building and back to Rockland, where tour instructions resume. Paths lead through the gardens, so explore at your leisure.

This Government House is the third on this 10-hectare (25-acre) site that commands a magnificent view over the Strait of Juan de Fuca. Government House I was Cary Castle, built by George Hunter Cary in 1860. Fined for riding his horse too fast over James Bay Bridge, and jailed for trying to fight a duel, he gave up on the colonies in 1864 and returned to England. The next owner sold the castle to the government, which used it to house the governor. The castle seemed to attract fires: a minor one in 1870 at the Queen's

Government House and its gardens.

Birthday Ball; one that burned down the coach house in 1872; and the final one that destroyed most of the building in 1899.

Government House II was completed in 1903, though the grounds were not designed until 1927. In 1957, this building also burned down. Government House III is the present one, containing just the porte cochère incorporated from the former building, though the style is much the same.

The main attraction for visitors here is the

grounds, which include a traditional Victorian rose garden with old-fashioned roses. Former Lieutenant-Governor David Lam spearheaded a move to restore and improve the grounds, which are now tended by enthusiastic and hardworking volunteers. Look for roses, bowers, beds of lavender and other perennials. Also in the gardens is a good variety of native and exotic trees, including Garry oaks, Douglas-fir, a weeping European ash and a fine tulip tree at the entrance gate.

Winter patterns on a Rockland Avenue house.

➤ When you leave the Government House grounds, turn right on Rockland.

Another clutch of heritage houses stands on these blocks of Rockland, a number of them no longer single-family residences, but divided into rental or condominium suites. The Arts and Crafts–style house at 1558 was built in 1904. Many Rockland and Oak Bay heritage houses follow Arts and Crafts precepts, which include an admiration of folk art and a nostalgia for medieval crafts, and characterized in architecture by such things as shingled walls and wood decoration. At 1442, built in 1912, is a California bungalow–style home adapted from the south; 1564, respite for the eyes because of its simplicity, a Georgian-style house from 1906; 1595 is Rappahannock, built in 1910, and, like many of its neighbours, commanding a view out over the distant water; 1617, another in Georgian style; and, 1648, Newholme, at the corner of Terrace Drive, an 1897 house probably designed by society architect Francis Rattenbury (see Oak Bay and James Bay tours for details of his life).

➤ Turn left on Terrace Avenue. This road is narrow and winding; it has no sidewalks. Exercise caution.

This narrow street is a delightful one, with turn-of-the-century houses, quiet gardens and Garry oaks. At 1001 Terrace is Buncrana, named for a settlement in County Donegal in Northern Ireland. Built in 1912 for former premier William Bowser, it contains about as many dormers and roof levels as architecturally possible. Check out the houses at 1000 and 1009 as well.

High above the heritage houses are two unexpected towers: one for water, one for apartments. The apartment building is the only high-rise to infiltrate Rockland. The 40-metre-high (130-foot) water tower was built in 1909 to ensure good water pressure for Victoria residents, a task it still occasionally fulfills for its neighbours in the Rockland area. For many years, it was topped by a neon light, rep-

This Edwardian-style house on Terrace Avenue was completed just before World War I.

This 1900 house on Terrace Avenue is in chalet Arts and Crafts style.

resenting a candle flame; floodlighting transformed it into a huge stone candle. That is no more, nor is the air raid siren installed during World War II.

A small park halfway along Terrace provides a place to sit and meditate on the good fortune of those who can afford to live in Rockland. Continue down the street to see a modern intrusion into the heritage landscape: you can further meditate on whether this blank-faced building is more attractive than its older neighbours.

> At the end of Terrace, turn left onto Oak Bay Avenue. At the next, X-shaped, junction, keep left onto Fort Street.

This route takes you past a few stores, where you can find a takeout drink or coffee, and on past 1501 Fort, the former home of newspaper owner and editor David Higgins. Higgins was probably the best example Victoria has ever seen of a crusading journalist, starting as a reporter when he arrived from Nova Scotia via California in 1858. Higgins has written much about this part of his life, and about the many colourful people he met along the way in British Columbia; some of what he writes is possibly even true. He was

bEST plAcES
to photograph flowers and trees:

Government House gardens. Tour 5.

Beacon Hill Park when the camas bloom in late spring.
Tour 4.

Fairfield streets when the trees are in bloom in early spring.
Tour 4.

Westsong Way, for the arbutus trees. Tour 3.

Rockland, for the Garry oaks. Tour 5.

University of Victoria Finnerty Gardens, when the
rhododendrons bloom, from April through June. Tour 7.

sued by a former premier, a suit he lost, the judge finding that he
had indeed libelled his opponent. He was sued for libel on other
occasions as well.

➤   Turn left on St. Charles Street.

The grounds of Illahie, at 1041 St. Charles, contain a number of
native and exotic trees. Illahie was designed in 1907 by prominent
Victoria architect Samuel Maclure. More mansions from around
the turn of the century are located at 1023, 1005, 944, 943, 914, 908
and 811 St. Charles. These blocks are particularly notable for the
variety of gates, fences and walls, in stone, wood and wrought iron,
that front the fine houses.

➤   Turn right on Rockland Avenue, to return to the starting
    point of the tour at the corner of Joan Crescent.

TOUR 6

OAK BAY

WHAT YOU'LL FIND:
Waterfront walking, heritage houses, pleasant residential neighbourhood, eclectic shopping in small neighbourhood shops. And tea, of course: this *is* Oak Bay. Though at last count, the coffee shops outnumbered the tea shops even here. Pity.

BACKGROUND:
Oak Bay has a reputation as the wealthiest and stuffiest part of greater Victoria, an honour at least partly due to its population being generally older and more British than elsewhere in the region. It's certainly still wealthy—Oak Bay's average income is a good third higher than in the rest of greater Victoria—but stuffy is disappearing as pubs, Italian delicatessens and sushi bars become part of the neighbourhood fabric.

In 1891, the Victoria Electric Railway and Lighting Company extended its streetcar lines to Windsor Park and Willows Beach in Oak Bay. That improvement in transportation underlay the birth of the municipality, as did the land boom of 1905 to 1912. In 1906, with 243 landowners in the area, Oak Bay was formally incorporated as a municipality.

Summer cottages were built not far from the end of the streetcar line, along the curving shoreline. Substantial houses were erected for the well-off and well-connected, and Oak Bay became, as it has remained, the most sought-after residential district, with the highest average house prices, in the region. A commercial strip developed along the main streetcar line on Oak Bay Avenue, but residents were determined that the area remain relatively genteel and free from alien activities. As you walk the streets of Oak Bay even today, you'll note the almost total absence of gas stations, fast food

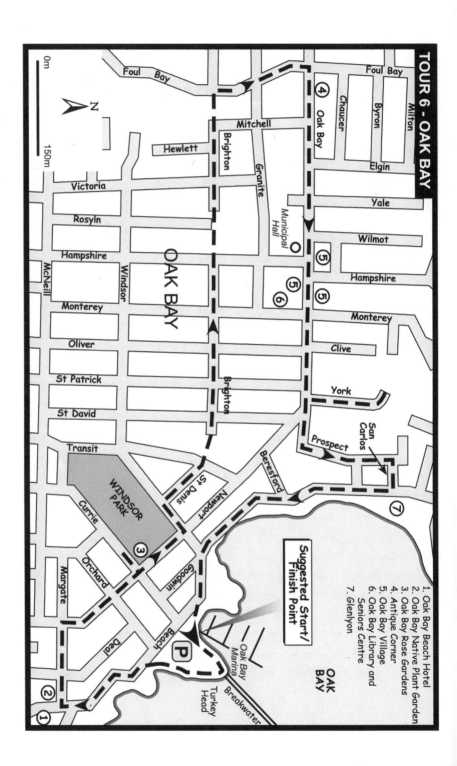

TOUR 6 - OAK BAY

0m
150m

N

Foul Bay
Milton
Byron
Chaucer
Foul Bay
Mitchell
Oak Bay
④
Elgin
Hewlett
Brighton
Granite
Yale
Victoria
Rosyln
Municipal Hall
Wilmot
Hampshire
McNeill
Windsor
⑤
⑤
Hampshire
Monterey
⑤
⑥
Monterey
OAK BAY
Oliver
Clive
St Patrick
Brighton
York
St David
Prospect
San Carlos
Transit
WINDSOR PARK
St Denis
Newport
Beresford
⑦
Currie
Orchard
③
Margate
Goodwin
Deal
Beach
P
②
①

Suggested Start/
Finish Point

Oak Bay Marina

OAK BAY

Turkey Head
Breakwater

1. Oak Bay Beach Hotel
2. Oak Bay Native Plant Garden
3. Oak Bay Rose Gardens
4. Antique Corner
5. Oak Bay Village
6. Oak Bay Library and
   Seniors Centre
7. Glenlyon

outlets and megastores. Not that Oak Bay flatly refuses to have fast food outlets within its borders, but it lets applicants know who makes the rules: McDonalds was told they couldn't have their golden arches, and KFC was refused its turning chicken bucket. McDonald's went elsewhere. KFC tried an Oak Bay location, but it's no longer in operation.

That resistance to change, now being echoed in other municipalities that have come to see the light (bigger isn't necessarily better) makes walking in Oak Bay a pleasure. Within a span of several kilometres (a few miles), you can summon the seals that live near the shore, catalogue native plants, admire sumptuous Edwardian architecture and browse through small shops with nary an international chain store in sight.

WATCH FOR:

Tweedy women with British accents; energetic groups of weekly walkers; store owners knowledgeable about their stock and happy to serve the customer; unusual, eclectic and frequently expensive things to buy.

TIMING:

An hour or two as a stroll, plus whatever time you choose to spend checking out Italian cheeses, left-handed widgets, nifty knick-knacks, tea and scones.

TO REACH THE ROUTE:

Since this is a circle tour, you can begin anywhere along the route. The best place for parking is along Beach Drive or in the parking lot at the Oak Bay Marina. Tour instructions begin from the marina, near the foot of Windsor Road. To reach the marina by car, follow Oak Bay Avenue to Newport, Newport to Windsor, Windsor to Beach, Beach to the marina—or follow Beach Drive and the other waterfront roads from downtown to Oak Bay for a waterfront excursion. Buses #1 Willows and #2 Oak Bay stop on Newport Avenue near the Oak Bay Marina, but if you are busing, you won't be worried about parking, so you can take any of the buses that go to Oak Bay Village (#1 Willows, #2 Oak Bay), and pick up the route there.

THE ROUTE:

➤ Begin at the Oak Bay Marina.

Back in 1893, the Mount Baker Hotel was built not far from here; a fine hotel, it was nonetheless too far from downtown to attract the customers it needed. It had its moments of glory, though. It could boast that the future King George V and Queen Mary and Prime Minister Wilfred Laurier stayed there in 1901. A year later, it was gone, burned to the ground.

The Oak Bay Marina was built in 1962, both as a marina and a tourist attraction. For several decades, crowds flocked to watch the

In Tilley hats and walking shoes, quintessential Oak Bay-ites enjoy the view near Turkey Head.

marine mammals at Sealand, and many Victorians remember being splashed by the antics of orcas and seals. Times change: Sealand's animals were sent elsewhere and the structure was torn down. Today, the marina is home to many millions of dollars worth of yachts and cruisers.

If you want to start your trip with a coffee infusion, try the marina coffee shop, on the lower level beside the moored boats. While you're down here, fending off the hungry crows that perch as close as they can get to the outdoor tables, look for the seals who make their homes under the ramp that leads to the boats. One or several will usually appear in the water to the left of the ramp. The seals aren't universally loved: at least one boat owner has been so startled by their sudden leaps out of the water that he dropped his marine wrench over the side. The marina is also home to a good restaurant that serves seafood, sushi and other items.

➤ From the marina buildings, follow the signposted pathway that curves around Turkey Head.

The point is named for a rock formation that no longer exists. This extended breakwater protects moored boats against most storms, though not all—when a severe southeaster breaks on this coast, it engenders waves and winds that can sink boats or toss them up onto the shore.

➤ When you reach Beach Drive, with the marina buildings on your right, turn left. Continue along Beach Drive until you reach the Oak Bay Beach Hotel.

Look offshore along here to see Jimmie Chicken Island, one of the islets across the bay. A group of Songhees native people lived on neighbouring Chatham in the 1880s and 1890s. Jimmie and Jenny Chicken lived alone on the island that now bears his name, fishing and selling produce to Oak Bay residents and the Mount Baker Hotel. When Jimmie died in 1900, hundreds of mourners arrived, some of them in more than 100 native canoes. He was buried on Chatham Island.

The first Oak Bay Beach Hotel was built in 1927. That building burned in 1929, and a new, very similar one was erected. In the lobby, you'll see some of the fine furnishings installed by the original owners. They travelled the world in search of antiques, brought them home and proceeded to sell them if any of their guests were interested: it wasn't unusual to see a price tag affixed to the underside of the table you had your tea on. Go upstairs to the Snug, the first and for many years the only bar/saloon/liquor lounge in all of Oak Bay, and one of the very few outside downtown Victoria. In those years, the Snug was a favourite haunt of UVic students. Now, hotel guests, visitors and locals compete for the tables on the balcony, which has one of the most peaceful sea views of any drinking establishment in the Victoria area.

➤ From the Oak Bay Beach Hotel, backtrack along Beach Drive a few metres, cross Beach Drive, and enter the Oak Bay Native Plant Garden on the corner of Margate Avenue.

This quiet corner is the result of a bequest from Ada Beaven. Arden, the attractive house celebrated architect Samuel Maclure designed for the Beavens, is long gone, and only this section remains of the gardens Maclure also designed.

➤ Follow Margate away from the water to Newport Avenue. Turn right. Follow Newport to Currie Road.

At 1052 Newport is the Tudor-style Oak Bay Guest House, built in 1912, and operating as an inn since 1922. It is one of a very few bed-and-breakfasts in Oak Bay, where zoning regulations are strict and rezoning permissions hard to come by. Original owner Bill Scott was known as the Oak Bay Philosopher; a man whose homespun wisdom was often found in the pages of the region's newspapers. The building at 1106 Newport went up in 1913, during Oak

Bay's building boom. The apartment building at 1147 Newport, known as Mount Baker Court, is unusual for the very small setback from the street, something unlikely to be allowed under today's building rules.

On the corner of Currie and Newport are the Oak Bay Rose Gardens, part of Windsor Park. The rose gardens were also the result of Ada Beaven's generosity; in 1937, she donated 500 rose bushes to establish the garden.

Stairs on a path along the walking tour route between the waterfront and Oak Bay Village.

➤ Turn left and walk a half-block up Currie.

At 2493 Currie, you'll see a vertically striped house that's a twin to the one across the park on Windsor Street. In 1926, Margaret Marsh separated from her journalist husband. Whether out of pique or out of love for her former home, Mrs. Marsh had this virtually identical house built on Currie Street. Mr. Marsh had other ideas: he promptly headed for Australia, returning years later to live on the Gulf Islands.

➤ Return down Currie, turn left on Newport along the park, and turn left on Windsor Road.

Take a look at the upper-middle-class houses that border the park, most of them built between 1910 and 1927.

➤ Turn right on St. Denis Street. Be cautious here: this street is narrow and has no sidewalks. At the end of the block, where St. Denis meets Transit, turn right, then immediately left on a narrow path (it can be muddy) that runs through the woods to the end of Brighton Street. Follow Brighton, crossing St. David Street and St. Patrick Street. Continue on Brighton, which looks more like an alleyway than a street in this next block.

Follow Brighton (it makes a few minor jogs) past Oliver and Monterey to Hampshire, where it temporarily ends. Across Hampshire, a path leads up a set of stairs; follow the path over the hill.

Beside the path and stairs is Insovenajh, a marvellous old stone house built in 1911 by an investment company, which then sold it to private owners. Now owned by a Victoria brew pub owner, it retains its slate roof and half-timbered gables. It's one of only two all-stone houses in Oak Bay.

➤ Continue down the hill on the path, then past Roslyn Road, which dead-ends on your left. Straight ahead is a narrow path that leads you to Brighton again. Follow Brighton to Mitchell Avenue, where the street ends. Follow the path straight ahead to Foul Bay Road. Turn right on Foul Bay. Follow Foul Bay to Oak Bay Avenue.

At the corner of Oak Bay and Foul Bay, Oak Bay Village's eclectic shopping begins. You might find a life-size bronze lady in one of the antique stores on the corner—or more standard antique furniture in walnut and mahogany. The specialty hardware store across Oak Bay provides such things as hand-painted house signs, while Ten Thousand Villages stocks crafts from around the world. A real feature of the block to the right is Charles Rupert, a shop that specializes in such things as William Morriss wallpapers, Liberty silk scarves and all that's necessary to refurbish the Arts and Crafts bungalows of Oak Bay. The store supplies furnishing for, among others, museums and period movie sets.

> ➤ From Foul Bay, turn right on Oak Bay, back towards the water. (Street numbers should be ascending.)

Two blocks of shopping are followed by two rather more nondescript blocks of apartment buildings and professional offices. The 1910 Edwardian bungalow at 2150 Oak Bay is one of the few houses left on this part of the avenue. Then the shopping begins again. Where you stop will depend on your tastes, but there's a great deal to choose from in this double line of small stores—no department stores or international chains here. Among shoppers' favourites: books, coffee, women's clothing, hardware, knitting wool, cheese, china, chocolate and candles. Oak Bay Avenue's first neighbourhood

A staff member displays wares outdoors at Foul Bay Road and Oak Bay Avenue.

Dickensian figures in Athlone Court.

pub, opening in 2001, was third-time lucky for would-be publicans: two other applications made over the years were turned down by Oak Bay council. But times have changed, and why not a pub, if Oak Bay truly strives for Englishness?

Just past the Municipal Hall on your right, before the corner of Hampshire Road, walk into the mews at Athlone Court, and look up at the top of the centre structure: carousel figures surround the clock in what must be Victoria's least-known piece of whimsical art. They were commissioned by the original owner of the restaurant in Athlone Court, then known as Pickwick's, and represent figures from Charles Dickens's *Pickwick Papers.* Once they were complete, the moulds from which they were made were broken, so they are unique. Once upon a time, they also revolved around the clock as it struck each hour, but that mechanism has long been broken.

The Castle Block, 2184–2194 Oak Bay, with its Tudor-style appearance, was built in 1936. The Oak Bay Theatre was a feature of this block for 50 years; it closed in 1986 and was converted into shops and offices. The red brick Bell Block at 2201 Oak Bay was built in 1913; check for the original owner's name in stained glass above the entrance to the apartments. The building that houses the Blethering Place, at 2250 Oak Bay, built in 1912 and therefore the oldest in the village, was first the home of a grocery and post office. The Tudor look is the result of a more recent facelift.

➤ Continue east on Oak Bay Avenue, crossing (if you haven't already) to the left-hand (north) side at Monterey Avenue.

You can stop for scones and tea at the Blethering Place, Victoria's original tea room (though you may find the ambience just too twee for words, the food is good and reasonably priced). Behind the tea room, off Monterey, is Monterey Mews, home to a traditional butcher's shop and half a dozen small shops.

➤ Continue east. Two blocks farther on, turn in to York Place, on your left.

Three streets run off Oak Bay Avenue, parallel to each other, from here to the waterfront: York Place, Prospect Place and Beach Drive.

At the turn of the century, two of Victoria's better-known architects bought six hectares (15 acres) of land here, subdivided, and began to design and build houses on the rambling view properties. A number still exist. Annandale, at 1587/1595 York Place, behind a stone wall on your right, was one of a set of identical twin houses owned by socially prominent Victorians. The other property has been torn down. This one was

The Blethering Place, in Oak Bay Village.

originally owned by Sir Charles Tupper, son of the Sir Charles who was a father of Canadian Confederation and, briefly, a Canadian prime minister. Annandale today has been divided into suites; barely visible behind the trees and brush, it has deteriorated over the years. The house at 1580 York, high above the street with a magnificent view out over the water, was built in 1906–7 for civil engineer Thomas Gore. The house at 1590 York Place, built in 1919 to a design by Francis Rattenbury, and the houses at 1605 York (1904) and 1630 (begun in 1907) are also of interest.

> ➤ Return back up York Place and turn left again on Oak Bay
> Avenue. Continue straight ahead on Oak Bay towards the
> water; don't take the curve onto Newport. At the end of
> Oak Bay Avenue, curve left onto Prospect Place, keeping
> a sharp lookout for errant traffic on this narrow street
> without sidewalks.

A number of the turn-of-the-century houses still command Prospect Place: the bungalow at 1660, originally built in 1899–1900 and

Behind bushes and trees stands Annandale, once the home of Oak Bay's most distinguished residents.

Now Glenlyon School, this mansion was built by soon-to-be notorious architect Francis Mawson Rattenbury.

somewhat altered; 1525 Prospect, 1908/1920; and 1535 Prospect, 1909. You can compare the house at 1513 Prospect with the main building of Glenlyon a block away. The smaller house was designed by architect Samuel Maclure for his colleague Rattenbury. Rattenbury was forced to give this lot and a house to his wife Florence as part of a hotly contested divorce settlement between two people who had grown to hate each other. But Rattenbury had no intention of designing his enemy's dwelling place, so Maclure did the job instead. Architectural historian Martin Segger commends this house for its "lack of ostentation," something no one ever accused Rattenbury of.

At the end of Prospect Place, at San Carlos Avenue, are five houses on Patio Court. With their towers and turrets and gables, they seem to belong in a fairy tale. They were built in 1927.

best places
with a village atmosphere:

Oak Bay Village, with a multiplicity of small specialty shops. Tour 6.

Sidney, where books, pottery, art and baked goods are all available. Tour 8.

James Bay Village, where young residents and old do their shopping. Tour 2.

Cook Street Village, for old movies and good coffee. Tour 4.

Cadboro Bay Village, for books, good cookies and unusual greeting cards. Tour 7.

➤ Turn right on San Carlos, to Beach Drive.

On the water side of Beach Drive is the house Francis Rattenbury built for himself in 1898, then added to in 1913–14. Rattenbury's story as architect, entrepreneur, wastrel and eventually murder victim is now well known. His house became a boys' preparatory school named Glenlyon, a role it still fulfills, though now for both boys and girls. If you walk along the beach, you can see the original house from the water side; you'll also see the coach house that once housed Rattenbury's Cadillac, dubbed Black Pearl.

➤ Continue along Beach Drive to the west, following the curve of the bay towards Oak Bay Marina, which you will see ahead of you, the starting point of this tour.

TOUR 7

UNIVERSITY–CADBORO BAY

WHAT YOU'LL FIND:
Gardens, totem poles, contemplative students; woods, coffee, food and drinks; books and beach walking.

BACKGROUND:
There aren't many universities with as pleasant a location as the University of Victoria. The 160-hectare (400-acre) site is bordered by wooded jogging trails and the forest of Mystic Vale. Just down the steep hill is Cadboro Bay, with its ocean beach and village shops.

The Cadboro Bay shoreline has long been inhabited. The Songhees native people lived here for centuries before the first European explorers arrived. When the Songhees moved to the area around Fort Victoria, the bay was for a time relatively deserted; it took a few more decades for people to decide that it would be pleasant to have summer cottages near the waterfront. The building of permanent homes took even longer, and depended on reliable roads and transportation to link the area to the rest of Victoria.

The area at the top of the hill was farmed for many years. In 1932, an airfield was developed here; from 1940 to 1943, an army camp occupied some of the land. Some 16 years later, Victoria College bought the camp and neighbouring land. Over the next decade, the University of Victoria was established here, and classroom and other buildings were erected.

A major feature of UVic was the circular road within which all academic instruction would take place. That feature still dominates the campus today. Though some academic buildings have spilled outside Ring Road, most are still contained within it, with residences and other buildings on the exterior. Though the buildings themselves are not always interesting—they lack

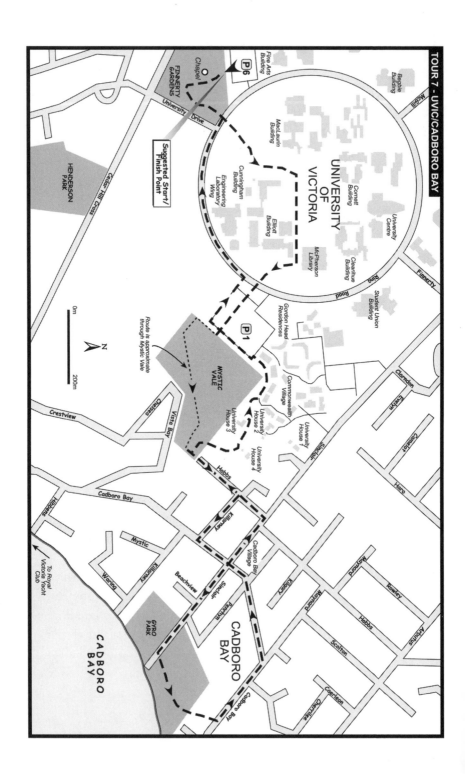

the character of older campuses—the green spaces lend a relaxed air to the university grounds.

WATCH FOR:
Horned owls, hundred-year-old rhododendron plants, interesting herbal scents on the air.

TIMING:
A 90-minute stroll; time added on for eating, drinking and sitting on the beach. One long set of steps down; one quite reasonable hill back up. Not suitable for bicycles.

TO REACH THE ROUTE:
This is a circular tour, so can be joined anywhere en route. If you're driving, head for the University of Victoria via any of the routes that lead to campus. From Ring Road, the road that circles the campus, enter Parking Lot 6, marked for the Fine Arts Building. Parking at UVic is free weekends and holidays, and after 6 p.m. weekdays. If you are driving to campus September through April, weekends and evenings are the best time to take this walk, since parking lots are jammed between about 8 a.m. and 4 p.m. during the university year. Or join the tour route at Cadboro Bay, parking in the beach parking lot. To reach the starting point by bus, get off any of the buses that go to UVic at the main UVic bus loop, and walk to the fountain in front of the McPherson Library, to pick up the tour there.

THE ROUTE:

➤ From Parking Lot 6, enter the University's Finnerty Gardens by walking past the chapel.

This interdenominational chapel was built in 1985, to provide a quiet and reverential space for students and others; it's a favourite for weddings and funerals.

Once you are in the gardens, paths lead you past hundreds of varieties of rhododendrons and other native and exotic species. You can wander as your will and horticultural interests lead you, bearing in mind that the tour will exit the gardens and enter the main part of the campus at a crosswalk just before Ring Road veers off towards University Drive and the city. The following route takes you more or less directly through the gardens.

➤ After you pass the chapel, take the path to your left. Keep straight on at the first Y, then bear right, keeping a cut-off tree to your left and continuing past a bench to a T-junction. Turn left, and follow a gentle S-bend along the path heading towards an arbour gate.

Finnerty Gardens were born of a donation by Cowichan Lake resident Jeanne Buchanan Simpson, who, with her husband, George, had created the largest collection of rhododendrons in British Columbia.

A student reads, surrounded by rhododendrons in the university's Finnerty Gardens.

It wasn't considered practicable to maintain the rhododendrons on site at Lake Cowichan. Instead, they became the nucleus of a campus rhododendron garden. First planted inside the Ring Road, the rhodos did not thrive in this damp site. A few were left where they were, but most were transplanted to the present site. Over the years, the gardens have been expanded, and an enthusiastic group of volunteers known as the Garden Friends, along with UVic gardeners, has spent thousands of hours developing and caring for them.

Rhodos are in bloom from January through June; April and May are the best times to tour. Some of the plants are now more than a hundred years old. Look for unusual forms on some of the oldest, most of which bear name tags of *R. decorum* or *R. fortunei*. After her husband's death, Simpson was unable to maintain her garden; struggling to compete against invading native plants, some rhodos grew into distorted shapes. The gardens now contain some 200 species of rhododendrons and azaleas, plus 1,600 trees and shrubs. Perennials and a variety of other native and exotic plants make this one of the most attractive gardens in Victoria.

➤ The path through the gardens takes you to Ring Road; a sign pointing towards the city centre should be on your right. Cross the road, and walk through the plant-covered arbour gate that spans the pathway opposite.
Bear right on the dirt/gravel path into a native plant garden, and continue through the gardens to a paved pathway. At the end of the garden, follow the paved path to your left.

This path takes you into the main area of campus buildings and the centre of the campus circle, where students lounge, throw Frisbees and contemplate nature, their studies and their relationships with their fellow students.

➤ Follow the path as it curves around, then turn right just past the fire hydrant on your right, keeping the totem poles on your left.

These totems are replicas of poles from the Tsimshian villages of Kitwancool and Gitlakdamiks, in northwestern B.C. between the Skeena and Nass rivers.

➤ Wander along this path towards a third, shorter totem pole, bearing left just before the pole and heading to the fountain you can see across the grass.

Details from a campus totem pole.
(Anton Studios)

This third pole pays tribute to the original Salish people of the Victoria area. The funds for the fountain, often a meeting or gathering place for students, were donated by philanthropists David and Dorothy Lam, to honour former UVic president Howard Petch.

Ahead of you is the McPherson Library. If it's open—and it usually is in daylight hours in regular or summer session—you could check in the entrance areas where works of art are often displayed. Or, if you have a sudden desire to discover more about astrophysics or 17th-century literature, you could wander over to the on-line or good old-fashioned wooden drawer card catalogues, then up the stairs to recreate your undergraduate days by slumbering in the stacks.

➤ Assuming you are still facing the library, head to the right, then to the left, passing between the library and the Elliott Building on your right. Turn right just past the Elliott Building and follow the path past the parking lot, keeping on the left of two parallel paths. Cross the Ring Road at the crosswalk and head for the back of the parking lot in front of you. Turn right on the gravel path and continue to the end of the parking lot.
Follow the path straight on until you see wooden stairs that descend into the vale. Follow the stairs down. Keep to the left at the bottom of the ravine, resisting the temptation to cross the wooden bridge and climb back up the other side of the vale.

You are now in Mystic Vale, a forested ravine that lies between the university and the community of Cadboro Bay. In the mid-1990s, great controversy ensued when the companies that owned much of the vale declared that they would develop the area for housing. Residents and others concerned about the natural and undoubtedly fragile area—because of its steep slopes—protested, holding at least one candlelight vigil in the vale. UVic eventually came to the rescue, finding $2.7 million from provincial and municipal grants and its own capital reserve funds to buy the 4.5-hectare (11-acre) property. Those who love the vale are torn: very relieved that it isn't a housing development, but a little disappointed by the way the university has sanitized it. The old mysterious and overgrown trails have been replaced by wooden staircases and a considerably cleaner forest. But it's still a favourite for walking, biking or jogging, and you'll sometimes see biology students, clipboard in hand, studying the 75 species of trees, shrubs, flowering plants and ferns. Come here just at dusk, and you may be lucky enough to hear the sonorous hoots of great horned owls that live in the vale, or perhaps even see one of the birds tucked motionless against a tree trunk.

Deep in Mystic Vale.

Though it's hard to be certain, it's possible that the name of Mystic Vale stems from a spring that rises in this area, location now unknown. In his book *The Mystic Spring and Other Tales of Western Life*, writer David Higgins (see Rockland tour) suggested that native people of the area thought the spring possessed medicinal properties. They also believed, he said, that if you looked into the waters of the spring during a full moon, you would see the face of the person who loved you reflected there. Childless women could become fertile by gazing into the spring. A large maple tree above the spring guarded the waters. Whatever the truth of the legend, the spring became a favourite place for Higgins and his friends to frolic.

➤ You will eventually emerge at the end of Hobbs Street in Cadboro Bay. Be polite here—the path is public, but the grass to your right is private.
Follow Hobbs to Killarney, and turn right. Follow Killarney to Cadboro Bay Road. Turn left, and enter Cadboro Bay Village.

This is one of Victoria's smallest and best villages. It's been kept small by the determined efforts of stubborn villagers who refuse to

Coffee outdoors in Cadboro Bay Village.

Walking the dog on Cadboro Bay beach.

believe that unrestrained development is good for you. You can stop for a coffee or a drink or a meal, read the real estate ads, buy an ice cream cone at the Cadboro Bay Market or a book at the Cadboro Bay Book Company. Olive Olio's serves good cappuccinos and lunches; the coffee shop across the street has a variety of coffees and snacks. After several good and not-so-good incarnations, Smugglers' Cove Pub has settled into reliably good service and food—sit on the outside patio and quaff a beer or sip a glass of wine. The pharmacy stocks Rogers' Chocolates and ankle bandages: your choice.

➤ Continue down Sinclair Road to Gyro Park and Cadboro Bay beach.

Take your shoes off, and shuffle in the sand (the area's dog owners are usually responsible about picking up after their pets). You can

bEST plAces
to view outdoor art:

Sidney, for the bronzed statues and wall murals. Tour 8.

Thunderbird Park, for the totems. Tour 1.

Westsong Way, for nymphs and nudes. Tour 3.

University of Victoria, for totems, statues and other art. Tour 7.

also try to spot Cadborosaurus Willsi, the mythical—or not, depending on your attitude to these things—sea creature that is said to reside in this area. Caddy was named in the 1930s by a news-paper editor who reported that a swimming serpent, otherwise known as a large marine cryptid, had been spotted off Cadboro Bay. Cadborosaurus is reported to be 5 to 15 metres (16 to 50 feet) long, with a flexible, snakelike body and a head that resembles that of a sheep, horse, giraffe or camel. It can swim along the surface of the water at a speed of up to 40 knots. You are most likely to catch sight of Caddy between October and April.

A representation of a Cadborosaurus is among the playground figures in Gyro Park behind the beach. Pretend you're six years old again and have your picture taken in the octopus.

You can walk the beach to the right at low tide all the way to the Royal Victoria Yacht Club, though you'll get quite muddy doing so. To the left and along to the east end of the bay is the 1,900-year-old site of a Songhees village occupied, when visitors called in 1839, by some 130 people.

> ➤ Turn left from the main path into the park/beach, and walk past the model Cadborosaurus. Follow a track across the grass to the left, then turn right on a paved path.

If you stray from these paths, you will probably get your feet wet. Before Gyro Park was established in 1954, this area was a marsh once popular with duck hunters. Ducks still paddle on small ponds here in winter and spring. It took many loads of wood chips to fill the swampy area and prepare it for seeding.

➤ Turn left on Cadboro Bay Road. Turn right on Sinclair and walk up the hill back to Hobbs. Turn left on Hobbs, walking back towards the Mystic Vale path. Turn right at the end of Hobbs onto a paved uphill path. You will emerge into a clearing; turn right on the paved road. Continue past a university house on your left, then up the paved road. At the top of the hill, keep left on the gravel path; university residences will be on your right.

In August 1994, athletes from 50 countries came to Victoria to compete in the Commonwealth Games. Among the facilities built for the games were these residences, townhouses that accommodate 376 students over the age of 20. In the summer, the Commonwealth Village Cluster operates as an inexpensive bed and breakfast for visitors to Victoria.

➤ Continue along this path to the far end of Parking Lot 1. Turn right along the edge of the lot and follow the path into the woods. At the first Y, keep left, to stay in the woods. Several minutes' walk along the path, when the Ring Road is in sight, turn right and cross the road.

Ahead of you is the Engineering Building. If you like, you can take a quick side trip to the front of this building, where you will find a cedar sculpture carved by Coast Salish artist Floyd Joseph. The 7.5-metre (25-foot) figure opens his arms in traditional fashion to welcome visitors to the university.

The Coast Salish welcoming figure at UVic. (Anton Studios)

➤ Follow the sidewalk along the side of Ring Road. In a few minutes, you'll see the main university entrance on your left, with a Y-shaped set of roads leading onto and off the campus. Just past the Y, cross Ring Road again, and re-enter the University Gardens on the signed path. Ahead is Lot 6, the starting point for the tour.

TOUR 8

SIDNEY

WHAT YOU'LL FIND:
Beaches, benches, bronzes, books and boats.

BACKGROUND:
Many of the suburban municipalities in metro Victoria are made up of large and newish subdivisions, where residents rely on shopping centres and megastores. Not Sidney. Established back in the 1890s, Sidney has steadfastly resisted these pressures, maintaining a low-rise downtown that relies heavily on local merchants. You won't find international chain stores here; when big-box retailers came calling, they were shown the door. Instead, Sidney has maintained a low-key, small-town Main Street—otherwise known as Beacon Avenue.

Transportation by water has long been a major factor in Sidney's fortunes. For about 30 years, a railway ran the 25 kilometres

Docks at Port Sidney.

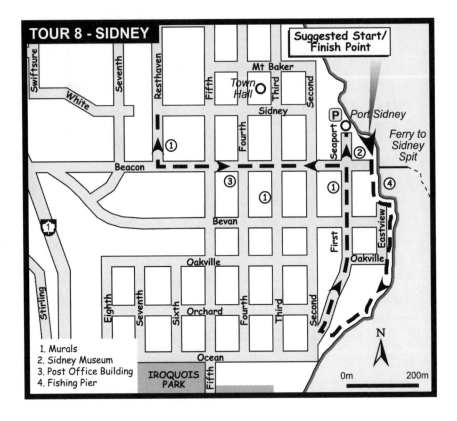

TOUR 8 - SIDNEY

Suggested Start/
Finish Point

1. Murals
2. Sidney Museum
3. Post Office Building
4. Fishing Pier

(15 miles) to Victoria; the steam train met the sternwheelers that served the Gulf Islands from the foot of Beacon Avenue. Over the years, ships sailed between Sidney and Bellingham, Nanaimo, Steveston and Anacortes. The ferries to the mainland moved to Swartz Bay, just north of Sidney, in the 1930s. The 1960s brought a government takeover of the ferries, and construction of a main highway from Swartz Bay to Victoria.

Determined not to be bypassed by highway traffic, Sidney has worked at developing its downtown as a destination. Among its visitor attractions: the Port of Sidney, a marina, restaurant and shopping development; a waterfront walkway; streetside murals and intriguing street sculptures; a variety of bookstores for books new and used.

WATCH FOR:

Sailboats offshore, fresh fish onshore, long-time Sidneyites chatting on the main street.

TIMING

A half-hour stroll that expands to half a day if you spend some time looking at the water, investigating the bookstores and stopping at the coffee shop, pub or restaurant. No hills.

TO REACH THE ROUTE:

If you are busing from the Victoria area, take the #70 Swartz Bay. Or if you want a slower country ride, try the #75 Central Saanich; it meanders through Brentwood and Central Saanich before finally arriving in Sidney. By car, take the Pat Bay Highway (#17) or any of the slower side-road routes to arrive at Beacon Avenue. Follow Beacon almost to the water; turn left on Seaport Place and park in the Port Sidney parking lot. Beware: they really do mean the two-hour limit.

THE ROUTE:

➤   Begin at the Port Sidney parking lot. Follow the walkway at the north end of the parking lot (beside Pelicanos coffee shop) down the gangplank for a look at the many and expensive boats that moor here.

The breakwater that protects the marina was first discussed in 1912, finally built in 1989. The 325-berth marina, completed in 1994, is privately owned—something of a continuing controversy in Sidney—and attracts fine and fancy boats from Vancouver, the American Pacific Northwest and from as far away as Hawaii.

➤   Return topside and follow the walkway left along the water, continuing to Beacon Avenue.

Bordering the walkway are a coffee shop, restaurants, a pub and souvenir shops, including one where you can pretend you are a kid again and pan for gold. Take a seat on one of the benches and enjoy the sunshine: Sidney boasts it is the sunniest and almost the driest place on the British Columbia coast.

➤   Turn left at Beacon Avenue, and walk out on the pier.

The government wharf has been located here since the turn of the century, with ships tying up alongside to take on the products of the neighbouring canning factory and sawmill. The cannery closed in 1922, the sawmill in 1934, but the wharf still sees some activity. A fish market at the end of the wharf offers whatever fish and shellfish are in season, sometimes right off the occasional fishboat that still ties up here. Check for smoked salmon or salmon candy you can munch as you continue the walk.

From mid-May to October, a ferry takes foot passengers on the

A Toronto tourist takes a break beside a permanent fisherman along the waterfront.

30-minute run to Sidney Spit provincial marine park just offshore, a pleasant round trip on a sunny day. From 1906 to 1916, Sidney Island was the location of a brick factory; it then became a "game preserve"—a private hunting reserve for affluent Victorians. The park on the spit end of the island has sandy beaches and warm water, and is a favourite camping, crabbing and picnic site. Whale watchers and kayakers also embark from the wharf for a trip on the waves.

➤ Return back down the wharf.

The pole at wharf end is topped by a replica of the beacon that appears on Sidney's town crest; it was built by local high-school students. Beacon Avenue takes its name from a beacon that could be seen on Sidney Spit, directly in line with the end of Sidney's main street. That landmark warned mariners of hazards in the area, though some say it was never lit. Sidney's motto translates as, "Let a beacon enlighten us." Since no beacon actually shines, is the town metaphorically in the dark?

➤ Turn left onto the seafront walkway.

Just past the beginning of the walkway stands the burnished carving of a diver. The carving was the 3 a.m. idea of Sidney hotel owner Denis Paquette. Created by artisan Al Porter from a six-metre (20-foot) red cedar log, it was erected on the beach in 1983 and later moved to its present location. Ahead on the left is one of Sidney's more recent sculpture series by artist Nathan Scott: a bronzed fisherman who sits with his tackle box on a bench near the fishing pier. You can walk out along the pier, recently restored as a place where children and other ardent fishers can drop a line—or a crab pot—into the water. A plaque on shore lists those who have contributed to this project. Just ahead and to the right, the top of a high spar is a favourite lookout for eagles. If you look higher up, you may well spot an airplane on a final approach to nearby Victoria International Airport.

➤ Continue onto Eastview Drive, then bear left on the Sidney Seaside Walkway.

This section of the pathway runs between rocky coves and new and expensive waterfront condominiums that cost their owners about half a million dollars each.

➤ Continue past the condos to the end of the walkway, which curves to the right and ends at First Street. Turn right on First and continue on to Beacon.

Just before Beacon, a wall mural on your left celebrates the past, present and future of ocean science and technology: take a look for the grey whale caught in a drift net and the deep-ocean vent chimneys, among other images.

➤ Turn left on Beacon Avenue and continue to Fifth Street.

Beacon is Sidney's main street, lined on either side with small stores that are mostly locally owned. On this, the south side, you'll find a

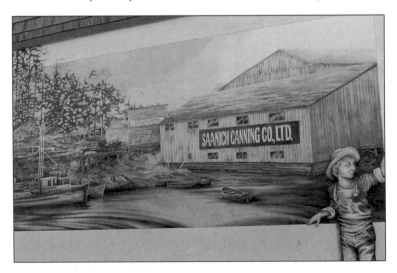

One of the new murals beside Sidney streets.

variety of restaurants, coffee shops and art galleries. Drop by old favourites the Sidney Bakery or Lunn's Pastries, Deli and Coffee Shop: pork pies, scones, and very good but very expensive chocolate.

To the left, just off Beacon on Third Street, check out the side of a building for the Saanich Canning Company mural that shows the old cannery in the 1920s. If antiques intrigue you: a block to the left of Beacon at Third and Bevan is a cluster of antique stores. You can investigate thrift and consignment shops on both Third and Fourth.

On Beacon between Third and Fourth is another of the downtown's statues created by Nathan Scott: the sou'westered Old Sailor, barefoot, with his wellie boots by his side. At the southwest corner of Fourth and Beacon is the revamped red brick 1936 post office, now incorporated into a retail and condominium complex, with a branch of the Sidney Museum in the basement.

Just to the left on Fourth is the Compass Rose, one of Sidney's many bookstores; it specializes in nautical books. Local bookstore owner Clive Tanner decided a few years ago to recreate Sidney as a Book Town, in the mode of other towns around the world officially recognized for their bookishness. Half a dozen stores, with used books and new, specialists or generalists, are clustered in the downtown area, a lure for bibliophiles from the Victoria area and elsewhere.

At Fifth Street, cross the street and continue west on Beacon for half a block or so, to Beacon Books and the Mystery Bookshop, two more of Sidney's bookstores.

➤ Walk to the corner of Beacon and Resthaven and turn right.

On the wall here is another mural, this one a bas-relief featuring 10 native paddlers in a dugout canoe, running through the reefs to escape a storm. Like the others, it is by Chippewa artist Chris Johnson (Ice Bear).

➤ Turn back to Beacon and turn left, to follow the street back down towards the waterfront.

Between Fifth and Fourth, you'll find Time Enough for Books, a used bookstore that specializes in fantasy and science fiction. At Fourth and Beacon is the original Sidney bookstore, Tanners—A Bookstore and More, with its extensive and eclectic selection of magazines, and Sidney's biggest collection of new books. Attached to Tanners is The Children's Bookshop.

Outside Tanners sits the town's most patient reader, book on her lap, handbag at her feet, another of the downtown's series of statues. Just up the street (to the north), in the parking lot of the local Army, Navy and Air Force Veterans club, are an F-86 Sabre fighter plane of Korean War vintage, a Sherman tank of the type used in the Second World War and the Korean War, and a navy gun from the deck of a ship, provenance unknown.

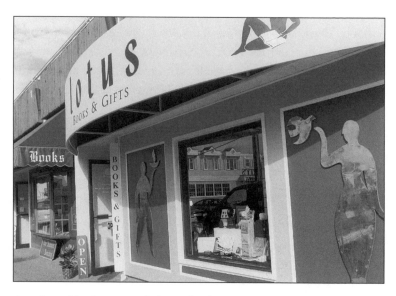

A variety of bookstores underlies Sidney's status as a Book Town.

> ➤ Continue along Beacon towards the waterfront.

On Third Street just to the left of Beacon are two more bookstores. The Haunted Bookshop has been a presence in the Victoria area since 1947, buying and selling antiquarian books in Victoria, then moving in the 1990s to Sidney. Look here for B.C. history. Next door is Lotus Books and Gifts, which advertises itself as "bright, beautiful and mystical" as well as consciousness-expanding.

At the corner of Beacon and Second, look for an anchor bolt embedded in the sidewalk and surrounded by chains. As the accompanying plaque explains, it's one of the bolts that anchored the cable stays for a travelling crane used to move lumber. The bolt is the last reminder of the sawmill that occupied this site for several decades.

> ➤ Continue across First Street and turn left.

The Sidney Museum here presents the history of the area, from Coast Salish through pioneer times, plus exhibits on the ecology of whales, sea lions, seals and sea otters. Open daily in summer; hours vary in winter.

➤ Continue along First Street to the Port Sidney parking lot and the starting point of the tour.

The scuba diver sculpture and condominiums near Sidney pier.

FURTHER INFORMATION

There exists a wide variety of books on Victoria and its neighbourhoods. Among those providing the best information on various features of the city, as seen on foot:

Exploring Victoria's Architecture, by Martin Segger. Victoria: Sono Nis, 1996.

Oak Bay's Heritage Buildings: More than Just Bricks and Boards, by Stuart Stark. Victoria: Hallmark Society, 1994.

Trees of Greater Victoria, by G.H. Chaster et al. Victoria: Heritage Tree Book Society, 1988.

Victoria Landmarks, by Geoffrey Castle and Barry F. King. Victoria: Sono Nis, 1985.

More Victoria Landmarks, by Geoffrey Castle and Barry F. King. Victoria: Sono Nis, 1988.

Victoria: Secrets of the City by Kevin Barefoot and the editors of *Monday Magazine.* Vancouver: Arsenal Pulp Press, 2000.

Websites:

www.oldcem.bc.ca is well worth a visit before you walk the Fairfield area, if you want to know the locations of specific graves of interest in Ross Bay Cemetery.

www.oakbaytourism.bc.ca has information on Oak Bay's history and shopping.

www.sidneybc.com and www.sidneybooktown.com have information on Sidney.

INDEX

Alexander Gray House 47
arbutus 67–68
Athlone Court 98
Avalon Road 42

Bank of British Columbia
  Building 18
Bastion Square 20–22
Battery Street 40
Bawlf, Sam 21
Bay Street Bridge 63
Beacon Avenue 117, 120–22
Beacon Books 121
Beacon Hill Park 65
Beaven, Ada 94, 95
Begbie, Judge Matthew Baillie 74
Belleville Park 47
Belmont Building 16
Bowser, William 86
Brighton Street 96–97
Brotchie Ledge 38, 69
Burnes, Thomas John 22

Cadboro Bay Village 110–11
Cadborosaurus Willsi 112
camas 77–78
Canoe Club 32
Capital Iron 31–32
carillon tower 34
Carr, Emily 41–42, 74
Cary, George Hunter 84
Cashman, Nellie 74
Cecilia Creek 61
Centennial Square 27

Charles Rupert 96–97
Chicken, Jimmie and Jenny 93–94
Children's Bookshop 122
Chinatown 29–31
Chinese School 28–29
City Hall 27, 28
Clover Point 76
Colonial Metropole Hotel 25
Commonwealth Village Cluster 113
Compass Rose 121
Cook, Captain James 13
Cook Street Village 71
Cosmos, Amor de 74
Craigdarroch Castle 81–82
Crystal Garden 11

Dallas Road 37–39
Douglas, Sir James 35, 47, 65, 74, 77
Dragon Alley 31
Dunsmuir, Robert and Joan 81–82

Eaton Centre 20
Emily Carr House 41–42
Empress Hotel 12–13

Fan Tan Alley 30
Finnerty Gardens (UVic) 105–7
Fisgard Street 28–31
Fisherman's Wharf 49–50
Fonyo, Steve 39
Fort Victoria 14–15, 103

Galloping Goose Trail 53, 60, 62
Garry oak 67–68, 85

Gate of Harmonious Interest
(*Tong Ji Men*) 30
Gatsby Mansion 47
Glenlyon School 101, 102
Goodacre Lake 68
Gorge Rowing Centre 61
Gorge waterway 59–60
Government House 84–85
Government Street 13, 15–20, 41–42
Gyro Park 111–12

Harrison Yacht Pond 39
Haunted Bookshop 123
Helmcken, John Sebastien 34
Helmcken House 34
Higgins, David 87, 110
Hudson's Bay building 28
Huntington Place 42

International Hostel Building 24

Jackson, George 47
James Bay Anglers' Association 50
James Bay Coffee, Books and
Internet Café 51
James Bay Inn 42
James Bay United Church 43–44
James Bay Village 43
Jimmie Chicken Island 93–94
Johnson Street 25
Johnson Street Bridge 33, 55

Lam, David 85, 108
Laurel Point 48–49
Law Chambers Building 22
Lekwammen 38
Lotbiniere Avenue 83
Lotus Books and Gifts 123

Macauley, William and Alexander 40
Maclure, Samuel 88, 94, 101
Maritime Museum of British
Columbia 21–22
Market Square 25–26
Masonic Temple 28
McPherson, Thomas Shanks 27
McPherson Library 108
McPherson Theatre 27
Memorial Crescent 72
Menzies Street Drill Hall 44
Mile 0, Trans-Canada Highway 40
Milne Block 26
Moka House 51
Morris Tobacconists 19, 20
Mungo Martin House 11
Munro's Books 19
Murchie's Tea and Coffee 19
Mystery Bookshop 121
Mystic Vale 109–10

Oak Bay Beach Hotel 93–94
Oak Bay Marina 91, 92–93
Oak Bay Native Plant Garden 94
Oak Bay Rose Gardens 95
Oak Bay village 96–99
Ocean Pointe Hotel 64
Ogden Point Café 52
Ogden Point docks 52
Olive Olio's 51, 111

Pantages, Alexander 27
Paperbox Arcade 25
Parliament Buildings 45–46
Pendray, William and Amelia 47–48
Pinehurst 40
Point Ellice Bridge 63
Point Ellice House 62–63

Point Hope Shipyards 63
Port Sidney 115, 117
Princess Mary 63
Prospect Place 100–1

QVs 51

Rattenbury, Francis Mawson 45, 86,
    100, 101, 102
Ring Road 107
Robertson II 64
Rogers, Charles and Leah 17
Rogers' Chocolates 17
Ross, Isabella 73
Ross Bay 76
Ross Bay Cemetery 72–75
Royal British Columbia
    Museum 34

Sail and Life Training 64
St. Ann's Schoolhouse 34
Salish 108
Sawmill Point 61
Selkirk Trestle 59–60
Selkirk Water 59
sequoias 83
Service, Robert 18–19
Shoal Point 50
Sidney Seaside Walkway 120
Sidney murals 120, 121
Sidney sculptures 119, 121, 122
Sidney Spit 119
Sidney Museum 124
Sidney wharf 118
Smugglers' Cove Pub 111
Songhees 103, 112
Spinnakers 57–58

Store Street 31–32
Strand Hotel 26
Swan's Hotel 32

Tanners—A Bookstore and
    More 122
Teague, John 28
Terrace Avenue 86–87
Thunderbird Park 11
Time Enough for Books 122
Torrefazione Italia 51
totem poles 11, 56, 78, 107–8
tourist information centre 14
trees: at Government House, 85
    at Parliament Buildings, 46
    in Beacon Hill Park, 67–68, 70
    in Rockland, 83, 88
    in Ross Bay Cemetery, 74–75
Turkey Head 93

Union Club 15
University of Victoria Chapel 105
Upper Harbour 63

Vancouver, Captain George 46
Victoria Conference Centre 12

Waddington Alley 24
Weiler Building 17
West Bay Marina 58
Westsong Way 55–58
Wharf Street 22–23
Williams, Michael 25, 32
Windsor Hotel 16

Yates Street 23–24
York Place 99–100